You are
My Beloved.
Really?

You are
My Beloved.
Really?

(compact version)

§

Harold G. Koenig, M.D.

ISBN-13: 9781530747900
ISBN-10: 1530747902

TO:
VETERANS AND
ACTIVE DUTY SERVICE MEMBERS

Acknowledgements:

§

THANKS TO ALL THOSE WHO CONTRIB-
UTED TO THIS BOOK IN A SPECIAL WAY

CHARMIN KOENIG
MICHELLE PEARCE
REBEKAH KOENIG
ENRIQUE FLORES
JORDAN KOENIG
MARTHA HALEY
MY FAITH COMMUNITY
MY PATIENTS

Contents

Introduction

Have you ever been someone's beloved? Many of us have never had that experience. We've heard about it and maybe longed for it. Perhaps we've given up the quest, given up on the possibility that we will ever be someone's beloved. But imagine if this were indeed the case. What if you were someone's beloved, but just didn't know it? What about God? Are you God's beloved? That **is** something to think about. But, how can we humans be loved by the Divine Being who created time and space, the earth, everything in the universe (including our bodies), and controls and keeps everything going?

But maybe God only loves certain people. Does God love everybody or only a chosen few? What about all the evil and suffering in the world? Doesn't that nullify God's love for us -- if God is really in control of everything? What if God doesn't even exist? All this might simply be wishful thinking, since we really don't know whether God exists or what he or she is like (I use "he" from here on because it's easier).

For now, let's assume that God exists and that we are God's beloved despite all the evil in the world...despite all the pain, trauma, and suffering that you, your loved ones, and your friends may have experienced. If we are God's beloved, what might our part be in this relationship? Is there anything that you or I can do to more fully experience that love and actually live every day as his beloved?

These are hard, complex and controversial questions. This little book attempts to answer (or at least struggle with) these questions. Although primarily for the Christian reader, the approach taken here also makes the book relevant to non-Christians and even to those who are not particularly religious. It's for anyone who has even the slightest leaning towards spiritual things, or believes there is something or someone out there.

This is also a personal book. I'm going to describe how I think God feels about us based on the evidence that I've dug up. I'm not a theologian or an ordained clergy, and so don't have any particular expertise or authority in theology. I'm just a regular guy. I've been trained as a physician and a scientist, and therefore spend most of my time doing objective quantitative medical research and training others to do the same. However, I'm not writing here from a scientific viewpoint. There is no scientific research that documents what I'm saying here, especially what I write about God. But this doesn't mean there is no evidence to back it up. Most of that evidence, though, comes from the holy writings of faith traditions passed down from generation to generation. By that I mean the Christian New Testament, the Jewish Bible, the Qur'an, and the Buddhist and Hindu scriptures. However, my scientific background does affect my approach to the subject. As a scientist I've tried to be as accurate as possible, and in the standard version[1] of this text, document everything.

Besides the sacred scriptures, the other evidence is more personal. It comes from experiences battling my own demons and, as a psychiatrist for over three decades, helping others battle theirs. Many, many lovely people have shared with me their pain and suffering over the years. I've even traveled with some to the very brink of eternity, to that river we must all cross over some day. I've promised several of these dear ones that I would see them on the other side. Many have become much more than just patients to me over the years. They have certainly been my greatest teachers.

When I refer to God here, I'm primarily referring to the Christian, Jewish, and Muslim view of

---

1 You are reading the "compact" version that has about 80% of the content of the "standard" version, but with most source citations removed to streamline it. Don't worry – the main points in the standard version are all here, and this compact version is also a bit easier to read and has pictures. The "standard version" with all source citations and expanded content is also available.

God – the one, Supreme God that members of these faith traditions believe in. However, a lot of what I say here also applies to anyone who believes in one overarching Divine Being. That includes those with a pantheistic view of God (which is a bit more complicated). If you don't believe in God, a higher power, or anyone remotely like that, and you are sure about it, then this book is probably not for you. In other cases, read on. The purpose here is to examine how God – if he does exist – feels about you and me. What is God like? Does God feel and care about stuff like we do? In particular, does he really *care* about us?

Perhaps he doesn't care. That would make sense based on all the pain and suffering many of us have been through. There are even some theological reasons for this view. The first century historian Plutarch argued that it was blasphemous to think that God was interested in human affairs. He portrayed God as far above the insignificant interests and pitiful struggles of people here on earth. Likewise, *deists* today believe that God's relationship to humans is not personal. They believe that God created the world and set it into motion, but otherwise doesn't want to get involved and doesn't really care what we do. Basically, we're here on our own. There are plenty of terrible things going on in the world today that justifies a rational person asking whether God cares. Does God give a hoot about what we want, or what we are doing to ourselves or to each other? Is he simply like an absent parent who's left his or her children to fend for themselves? Perhaps…perhaps not.

Here is a brief summary of what you are in for. Each of the 24 chapters is short and emphasizes a specific point. The first chapter describes what I mean by the title of this book. It examines where I got this maybe silly notion that we are God's beloved. In the second chapter I acknowledge some unpleasant facts about the world. Indeed, reality cannot be ignored. In the third and fourth chapters I examine whether God exists and what he might be like. In the fifth chapter, I explore why God allows so much evil and suffering in the world, when he could simply do away with it (i.e., get rid of evil; he tried getting rid of people with the Flood, but that didn't work). In the sixth chapter, I examine the real cause of evil.

Chapters 7-11 lay out the evidence supporting God's love for Christians, Jews, Muslims, Buddhists, and Hindus. These chapters are important in determining who exactly God loves, if anybody. In chapter 12, I examine how God feels about a particular group of people, Veterans and active duty Service Members. In chapter 13, I describe different ways that God might love us, and in chapter 14, address why we might have trouble feeling God's love (even if God really exists and really loves us). The next eight chapters focus on practical steps necessary to fully experience God's love and favor. The book concludes with a bit about me the writer, and a few final comments.

Bear in mind one thing. You *already know* most of what you will read here. I'm not presenting anything new. I'm just reminding you of things and connecting them together to figure out how God feels about us. Knowing how God feels about us, I think, is important.

So, find a quiet place, get settled in, and let's get started.

CHAPTER 1

You are My Beloved

Soon after I wake up each morning, I read a short passage scribbled on a piece of scrap paper: "You are my Beloved. My favor rests on you." The full passage is:

> *Many voices ask for our attention. There is a voice that says, 'Prove that you are a good person.' Another voice says, 'You'd better be ashamed of yourself.' There also is a voice that says, 'Nobody really cares about you,' and one that says, 'Be sure to become successful, popular, and powerful.' But underneath all these often very noisy voices is a still, small voice that says, 'You are*

my beloved, my favor rests on you.' That's the voice we need most of all to hear. To hear that voice, however, requires special effort; it requires solitude, silence, and a strong determination to listen. That's what prayer is. It is listening to the voice that calls us 'my beloved.'

When I first read that, I wasn't so sure I was God's beloved. I haven't experienced any major trauma or abandonment that would cause me to feel rejected, alone, unloved, or unlovable. But I still had doubts about how God felt about me. Even today, after repeating this statement every morning for years, I soon forget as the day progresses. So I have to frequently remind myself: "You are my beloved."

The full quote above is taken from *Bread for the Journey: A Daybook of Wisdom and Faith* by Henri Nouwen (1996, HarperOne). Nouwen was a professor and theologian at the University of Notre Dame and at Yale and Harvard universities. Despite his fame and academic reputation, however, he chose to spend his final days living and working with the mentally and physically handicapped at the L'Arche Daybreak community in Richmond Hill, Ontario. He died in 1996, the same year the book above was published. The quote is actually an elaboration of a passage in a book he wrote for a Jewish friend, titled *"Life of the Beloved: Spiritual Living in a Secular World"* (Crossroad, 1992), heralded as his most important contribution.

Nouwen insisted that God loves us and that all of us are "favored." He believed that God welcomes every person, whether they believe in him or not. None are excluded. But how can "favor" mean anything if everyone has it? Favor is not fair. It means someone is getting more of something than others. Favor often involves being preferred before doing anything to deserve it. Nevertheless, Nouwen believed that God's favor is available to all, whether they realize it or not. Realizing it, though, makes a difference he thought.

But how can we all be blessed and favored when there is so much evil in the world? Many do not feel loved or favored by any person, and

certainly not by a divine being. It is indeed difficult to make sense of the assertion that we are all
loved and favored by God.

CHAPTER 2

When Nothing makes Sense

§

GOD IS SUPPOSED TO BE omnipotent (all powerful), omniscient (all knowing), omnipresent (everywhere present), and in control of everything. If that is true, *why* does God allow seemingly unbearable suffering and incomprehensible evil? It is a simple question that deserves a simple answer. Who can deny the horrific evils that have taken place and are taking place all the time? Just watch CNN or Fox News. Consider the following events that have taken place over the past one or two generations.

Look at what happened to the Jews in Europe prior to and during World War II. The Jews, according to the Bible, are God's "chosen people."

However, nearly 6 million were murdered during the Holocaust from 1933 to 1945. Men, women and children suffered terribly during their last days from beatings, torture, exhaustion, starvation, or incineration in the furnaces of concentration camps like Auschwitz-Birkenau. In addition and often ignored, are the more than 5 million non-Jews murdered by the Nazis during this time (many killed for trying to help Jews escape). If a loving caring God existed, one who is in control, how could he let this happen to no less than his *chosen people*? The senselessness of that event is one reason why many Jews today no longer believe in God and why Europe has moved so rapidly towards secularization in the latter half of the 20th century.

As bad as the Holocaust was, those deaths are dwarfed by the more than 8,500 children under age 5 who die *every day* from malnutrition or hunger-related causes. That means over 3 million children die from hunger every year (36 million over a 12-year period like the Holocaust). What about the nearly 800 million malnourished children and adults in the world in 2015, many of whom will die from diseases related to inability to access enough food? Can we put that on God too? Nearly all those deaths could be prevented by people in wealthier countries sharing their resources with the poor. According to a report from the Global Burden of Disease Study published in the medical journal *Lancet*, obesity is now killing three times the number of people that starvation is killing. Rather than God being responsible, aren't all the good and decent people in the world who are not starving (including me) responsible for that? I'm just asking.

The widespread evil in the world does not stop here. ABC News reported that 400,000 people die from violent deaths every year as a result of war. The United Nations indicates that nearly 500,000 people die yearly from intentional homicides resulting from crime, drug use, or domestic violence. In the Middle East and Africa, nearly 20,000 civilians are killed every year by ISIS, Boko Haram, and other terror groups. If God exists and is loving or caring, how could he allow such things to happen? Is there any wonder why many question God's existence, and perhaps even conclude that it is better not to believe in God than to believe in a God that allows all of this?

In the opening sentence of *The Road Less Traveled*, psychiatrist M. Scott Peck makes a profound statement. He says: "Life is difficult." He saw this first hand as he cared for people during the most desperate and stressful times in their lives. I've seen it too. There are terrible things that happen, and those terrible things are not equally distributed. Some people must endure more hardship than others. And it's not always their fault. Some call it "bad luck."

Personally, I believe everything has a purpose. What that purpose is, however, is sometimes hard to figure out. Recently, I've been grappling with an experience that has challenged my understanding. My wife, who has a strong religious faith and cares deeply about others, has for years experienced chronic pain. That pain has worsened over the past two years due to an autoimmune disorder. Pain in her knees, hips, and shoulders has led to multiple major surgeries (at least a dozen by now), and she is at a point where they say nothing more can be done. She is left with daily pain, sometimes shockingly severe. She has difficulty exercising, trouble standing and walking, and is experiencing increasing numbness in her arms and legs (alternating with that intolerable pain). All of this is terrifying to her and me. The best doctors at Duke University Medical Center say they can't do a thing about it. I've become overwhelmed at times because I can't do anything to relieve this dear, precious lady's distress. I don't understand why God, if he is all powerful and in complete control of everything, allows this uneven distribution of good and bad. It doesn't seem fair – at least on the surface of things (and pretty far down below the surface as well).

Before trying to understand why God allows evil and why bad things happen to good people, we need to first address the basic question of whether God exists or not, and if he exists, what kind of God he is.

CHAPTER 3

Does God Exist?

§

THE FIRST STEP – determining whether God exists
or not – is pretty important. Brother Lawrence, a
17th century monk, described how he dealt with this
question:

> I set out first, to think through his divine exis-
> tence – that he really and truly and objectively
> **exists**, as Someone quite other and apart from
> me, his creature. That was first, and I thought
> of him and all I knew of him from the Scriptures
> and in my experience until I was totally convinced
> that God **is**. I had no intention of spending my life

> *in the presence of a Being who was simply a fig-*
> *ment of my imagination.*[1]

According to Gallup Poll International, 89% to 98% of the world's population believes in God. Most of the 2-11% of people who don't believe come from communist countries such as China and North Korea where religion has been discouraged or outlawed for decades. Indeed, 76% of the atheists in the world reside in Asia or the Pacific. In the U.S., only 5% say they are "convinced" atheists and an additional 5% say they don't know (or didn't respond). Of the remaining 90%, about 20% believe in some kind of higher power or divine being and the majority (70%) believes in a personal God.

By "personal God," I mean that God is a person, *a real person*. He is like us. He has feelings, positive and negative ones. According to the Judeo-Christian scriptures, we were created in God's

---

1 Winter D (1971). *Closer than a Brother.* Wheaton, IL: Harold Shaw Publishers, p 50

image and likeness (Genesis 1:26). God, however, is different than most people we meet and interact with, since we can't physically see or touch him. So, that leaves open the possibility that we are simply imagining him. God could be a psychological projection of an all-powerful parent figure, or just a result of wishful thinking. Freud described belief in God as an "illusion" (a false idea or belief based on a misinterpretation of the senses).

In contrast to Freud, Sir John Templeton – a very successful Wall Street investor and multi-billionaire – came to believe that God was not only real but the only reality that exists.[2] He argued that the illusion was actually *this world* and all the petty problems that we struggle with and put such a high value on. He may have a point there. Is it rational to believe that our true identity as a human is a biological organism without meaning or purpose, existing only momentarily on the eternal timeline of an infinite, merciless universe? Are

---

2 Templeton JM (1994). *Is God the Only Reality?* Philadelphia: Templeton Press

we simply animals whose sole purpose is to propagate our species, animals that are slowly evolving into organisms that will look completely different from us in a few million years? Despite my extensive knowledge of science, physics, and evolution, that just doesn't make sense to me.

Some have even challenged the notion that rational thinking is always the best way to arrive at the truth. World War I British chaplain Oswald Chambers says that "belief" in God is not an intellectual act at all, but a moral act. It is about *my will*, something I consciously and deliberately decide on and commit to. That moral act, then, leads to belief. However, it's not only about my will and choice, says Chambers. God plays a part too – the first part.

> *I am introduced into the relationship by the miracle of God and my own will to believe, then I begin to get an intelligent appreciation and understanding of the wonder of the transaction.*[1]

1 Chambers O (1935). *My Utmost for His Highest*. Uhrichsville, OH: Barbour Publishers, 2000, December 22

Thus, in my somewhat biased opinion (and that of most of the human race), I think the evidence favors a decision to fling oneself on believing in God and basing life on that – betting that God really exists and more than just existing, that he really cares about us. Yes, maybe that's an illusion. But even so, living in a world where God is personal, available, and cares, sounds a whole lot better than the alternative. The alternative is living in a world where you've only got yourself to rely on or other people just as helpless and powerless as you are.

One reason for resistance to believing in God is what it means if God really does exist. This is particularly true if God wants to be involved in humanity and cares about what we do. We all have an intense desire to direct our own ships, control our own lives, and do whatever we want to do (Adam and Eve's problem too). If God really exists, then we'd probably have to think and act differently. If he doesn't exist or doesn't care, then we're free to live and act however we want to maximize our pleasure during these short meaningless lives.

But, what if God does exist? If so, we need to know what kind of God he is and what he might expect from us.

CHAPTER 4

What is God Like?

§

THE VAST MAJORITY OF HUMANITY has come to the conclusion that God exists and is very real – not some imagined being or illusion. There is also the belief that he is personal, not some vague or distant being who is unconcerned, uninvolved, or unavailable (as deists believe).

Of course, no one knows for sure whether God exists or what he's like since nobody's ever seen him or come back from the dead to report on him. However, many believe that the one characteristic best describing God is that he is *good*, purely and completely good. It is from that goodness that his love comes and his desire for our good. Supporting that, here are some characteristics of God based on the Judeo-Christian scriptures.

God describes himself to Moses as:

> *The Lord, the Lord, the compassionate and gracious God, slow to anger, abounding in love and faithfulness, maintaining love to thousands, and forgiving wickedness, rebellion and sin.* (Exodus 34:6-7)[1]

The Tanakh (Jewish Bible or Old Testament) emphasized God's power and justice, as well as his love and forgiveness. The New Testament does likewise, but stresses God's compassion and mercy. Christians believe that the best evidence of what God is like comes from the person of Jesus. The apostle Paul said that Jesus is "the image of the invisible God" (Colossians

---

1 Except where specified, all Bible verses cited here are from the *New International Version* (NIV) of the Holy Bible. Grand Rapids: Zondervan, 1978.

1:15) and the "exact representation of his being" (Hebrews 1:3).

Therefore, it might help to examine what we know about Jesus. We know that he was a man with lots of emotions. Jesus experienced the emotion of love. He loved his disciples (John 13:1) and even washed their feet (John 13:5). Jesus also had some emotions that weren't so pleasant. He wept at the tomb of his friend Lazarus (John 11:35) and cried over his rejection by the Jewish people (Luke 19:41). He suffered (1 Peter 2:21; 1 Peter 3:18), was tempted (Hebrews 2:18), and got angry (Matthew 21:12-13; Mark 11:14). He felt betrayed by some of his closest friends (Matthew 27:3; Luke 22:56-60), and even felt deserted and forsaken by God himself (Matthew 27:46). In Isaiah's prophecy, he describes the Messiah as "a man of sorrows, and acquainted with grief" (Yeshayahu 53:3).[2] Christians believe that he was describing Jesus. Thus, from this description of Jesus, one might conclude that God experiences

_____

2 All quotations of Jewish scriptures are from the *Jewish Publication Society Bible* (http://www.breslov.com/bible/)

emotions, including sorrow, anger, and love – just like we do. I think God experiences his greatest sorrow when we suffer as a result of wandering off the path that he knows best for us, or when we experience sorrow and suffering from painful situations that are not our fault.

There is also the belief that God is constantly reaching out to make contact with us. This aspect of God, i.e., his desire to communicate and make contact, was recognized centuries ago by Michelangelo in his painting of the Sistine Chapel in Rome, Italy (1508-1512). Notice in the painting how God is straining to touch the hand of man. Man, in contrast, appears seated and only half-hearted as he reaches out to touch God's outstretched hand.

Islam likewise emphasizes God's desire to reach out to humans.

> *He who draws close to Me a hand's span, I will draw close to him an arm's length. And whoever draws near Me an arm's length, I will draw near him a fathom's length.[1] And whoever comes to Me walking, I will go to him running.* (Hadith Qudsi 110, No. 1)

---

1 The distance, fingertip to fingertip, created by stretching one's arms straight out from the sides of the body

In Jesus' parable of the prodigal son, the father (representing God) comes running to meet the son (representing us):

> *But when he was yet a great way off, his father saw him, and had compassion, and ran, and fell on his neck, and kissed him.* (Luke 15:20)

Jesus, whom Christians believe to be God, expresses sadness about people's lackadaisical attitude towards him.

> *Jerusalem, Jerusalem, you who kill the prophets and stone those sent to you, how often I have longed to gather your children together, as a hen gathers her chicks under her wings, and you were not willing.* (Matthew 23:37)

So what is God like, besides being omnipotent, omniscient, omnipresent, and in control of everything? I believe he's personal and reaching out to us – like a close, close friend, one who knows we're in trouble.

One who has unreliable friends soon comes to ruin, but there is a friend who sticks closer than a brother. (Proverbs 18:24)

CHAPTER 5

Why does God Allow Evil?

§

THERE ARE FORCES OF DARKNESS out there whose intentions are not good (assuming, of course, that there is any intention behind them at all). You can call those dark forces bad luck, evil, the Devil, or whatever you like. I'm going to call them *evil* here, since this is a commonly known term. The fact of evil has to be acknowledged and reckoned with. Everything in this world is simply not good. A lot of it is good, but definitely not all of it.

Life is hard, as psychiatrist Scott Peck said, and often makes very little sense. As I mentioned in Chapter 2, the situation here on earth doesn't speak favorably for an all-powerful, ever-present, all-knowing, completely good Creator, who apparently allows terrible things to happen -- including things he could prevent. As a result, you may have concluded that it proves there is no God or at least not a God who cares about you or me. You may have concluded that there is no purpose to anything, and that events are simply random, a result of brutal evolutionary forces in nature that seek to weed out the unfit among us. For some, this view may actually be more comforting than belief in an all-powerful God who could prevent bad things, but doesn't.

Even worse, you may have decided that whoever created this world is a tyrant, vindictive, ready to punish you for the slightest offense -- out to spoil your fun, take away your pleasure, and trap you in your mistakes. This could easily make you feel that God, if he does exist, is unfeeling, simply a law enforcer, with no regard for you as an individual. You feel cursed, abandoned in a loveless, cold world.

If you feel this way, you're not alone. Many have these thoughts and feelings. The problem, though, is if you get stuck there. Those feelings of alienation from God can destroy you. That is guaranteed (and backed up by a lot of research). Better not to believe in God than to believe in this kind of God.

But, let's get back to the original question (sometimes called the problem of *theodicy*). Why does a loving God allow evil to thrive and bad things to happen that deeply hurt us? Doesn't sound like love to me. I'm sure you've heard the following attempt to explain evil, but here it is again.

The presence of evil in this world doesn't prove that God doesn't exist or doesn't care. In fact, it proves the opposite. It proves that God loves us and desires to be *freely* loved by us. Have we not been given the greatest privilege of all? That privilege is the freedom to choose to love or not to love. We are not just animals controlled by natural instincts over which we have no control. As humans created in God's image we have something that animals don't. It is that wonderful freedom to choose. Without that freedom, love wouldn't mean a darn thing. Imagine if we didn't have the freedom to choose, and always did the right, loving thing. How would we be different from a machine or a mindless robot? What if your friend or spouse had to love you and couldn't do otherwise? Would that be a real friend? Would that be love? Love could not exist without the freedom to *choose not to love*. It is precious only because we have the freedom to choose not to. It is the priceless gift that makes us truly and distinctively human, *and like God the creator*.

Something happened, though, as a result of this great gift. Along with the freedom to choose came the choice not to love God and the temptation to go a way different from God's way. Eve chose to eat the forbidden fruit in the garden, despite God's warning: "But of the tree of the knowledge of good and evil, thou shalt not eat of it: for in the day that thou eatest thereof thou shalt surely die" (Genesis 2:17, KJV). The Devil countered with a temptation: "For God knows that when you eat from it your eyes will be opened, and you will be like God, knowing good and evil" (Genesis 3:5).

Well, Eve got exactly what the Devil promised her. Henceforth came into human consciousness the knowledge of good (God's way) and evil (not God's way). Adam chose to eat the fruit that Eve offered him, knowing it was not God's way. Cain chose to kill his brother out of jealousy for him, knowing it was not God's way.

All of us have been following our own way from birth onward, concerned first and foremost with meeting our needs in our own way, not wanting to be limited or restricted or told what to do. This fact cannot be denied. We are primarily interested in our own needs, pleasures, and security -- often trying to dominate and control others to get those needs met. Indeed, the common occurrence of war, murder, theft, lying, cheating, greed, impatience, desire to seek retribution, etc., testifies to this reality. Physicist and world renowned atheist Richard Dawkins called it the "selfish gene" – the natural inherited tendency for humans to be self-centered.[1] This doesn't mean that we don't sometimes rise

---

1 Dawkins R (1990). *The Selfish Gene*. NY, NY: Oxford University Press

above our preoccupation with self. We call people who sacrifice themselves for others "heroes" and give them medals for valor. We admire and respect them because it is not the norm. We all have that potential for heroism, but it is not the norm.

So, God created humans in his image and likeness with the ability to choose -- free will -- and he put us in charge of everything he created. Not only were we created at the center of it all, but also as *part of it*. The consequences of human disobedience, then, were devastating. The evil that resulted from the freedom to depart from God's will was not limited to humans alone, but became imbedded in the natural world itself. Recall the initial act of creation. God described creation as good -- all of it -- and not only good, but "very good" (Genesis 1:31). That has changed.

Now, the natural universe is in a process of decay and death (as God warned in Genesis 2:17). Within the science of physics this process is called "entropy" (and reflects the second law of thermodynamics). Entropy describes the tendency of nature to deteriorate towards maximum disorder in any isolated system. The entropic principle means that the world and universe is constantly moving from a state of order to a state of disorder. The results are natural disasters, hurricanes, tornadoes, and the release of decay more generally in the form of inherited and acquired diseases, accidents, pain and death. The original creation had none of these. Before the "fall," Adam and Eve walked and talked with God. They were told to be fruitful and multiply and were charged to restrain and care for all that God created:

> *And God said, Let us make man in our image, after our likeness: and let them have dominion over the fish of the sea, and over the fowl of the air, and over the cattle, and **over all the earth**, and over every creeping thing that creepeth upon the earth... And God blessed them, and God said unto them, Be fruitful, and multiply, and replenish the earth, and **subdue it**...* (Genesis 1:26, 28, KJV).

Yes, things have changed. The freedom to choose includes the choice to ignore God and not believe in him at all. It includes the decision to ignore the needs of others worse off than we are or take advantage of them. It includes the harm that people may have done to you, intentionally or not. You may have been hit by a drunk driver. You may have had parents or relatives who abused you, leaving a crippling physical or emotional scar. You may have been injured by severe weather, or developed a disease or illness that causes pain or disability. You may have lost a beloved child, brother or sister, or dear friend due to an illness or accident. You may have had to sit by helplessly and watch a loved one suffer. You may have been born in a war-torn, poverty-stricken area of the world, where you and your family had to struggle to survive.

Most if not all of these things you had no control over and could not have prevented. This is all the result of the freedom that exists within the very heart of the natural world that involves a certain freedom to go wrong – the departure from perfect obedience to God's will that existed in all of creation at the beginning.

CHAPTER 6

The Cause of Evil

§

WALT KELLY IN THE COMIC strip *Pogo* said "We have met the enemy and he is us." Looking for the cause of evil? There it is. Evil results from our decisions today and the decisions made long ago by our ancestors. The decisions we make affect others, and we are affected by others' decisions. The results of those decisions trickle down across the generations. Seventeenth century English author John Donne said "no man is an island." Here is the full quote:

> *No man is an island entire of itself; every man is a piece of the continent, a part of the main;*

if a clod be washed away by the sea, Europe is the less, as well as if a promontory were, as well as any manner of thy friends or of thine own were; any man's death diminishes me, because I am involved in mankind. And therefore never send to know for whom the bell tolls; it tolls for thee.[1]

Have you ever considered that the 10 Commandments were given to protect us, not ruin our fun? The word "sin" is derived from a Hebrew word that means "to miss the mark" (an archery term). When we sin, we miss the target that is our greatest good. If God loves us, then it is perfectly understandable why he hates sin. Why? Because of the pain and suffering it causes us. Wouldn't you hate anything that harms those you love? First, sin prevents us from perceiving God's love. God's love can't get through because sin blocks it. Second, sin hurts us and everyone around us whom God loves. Is that so surprising? How do we express our love

---

1 Donne J (1624). *Devotions Upon Emergent Occasions* (Meditation XVII). London: A. M. for Thomas Jones

for our children? Most of us want our children to live full, successful and happy lives. Maybe God wants the same for us. Perhaps he knows that sin prevents happiness, and results in anxiety, sadness, and despair.

Failure to follow the rules that God established to preserve our happiness (i.e., the "moral law") -- <u>always</u> results in pain and suffering, either now or later. Sadly, this also applies to not following God's rules when responding to bad things that happen to us *despite no fault of our own*. In some cases, despair or anxiety has nothing to do with our actions, but rather stems from biological or inherited causes. Even when we are feeling sad, depressed or anxious simply because of our biology, departure at any time from these rules, whether you call them laws, morals, values, or ethics, results in trouble.

If we get away with it initially, sin predisposes us to act in a certain way that leads to trouble later on. The person who steals and gets away with it will steal again, and again, and again, until he is caught. There is nothing that can prevent the consequences of breaking the rules that ruthlessly govern human behavior. In *The Sovereignty of Ethics*, Ralph Waldo Emerson (American essayist, lecturer, and poet) describes the natural law in this way:

> *The law is: to each shall be rendered his own. As thou sowest, thou shalt reap. Smite, and thou shalt smart...if I violate myself, if I commit a crime, the lightning loiters by the speed of retribution, and every act is not hereafter but instantaneously rewarded according to its quality.*[1]

The opposite occurs when we follow God's rules. Those who believe in a personal God believe that he wants us to love him and to love others in the same way that he loves them. Emerson says when you do this, nothing can stop good things from happening:

---

1 Emerson RW (1878). The sovereignty of ethics [from Emerson's Lectures and Biographical Sketches]. *North American Review* 10(12): 175-206

If you love and serve men, you cannot, by any hiding or stratagem, escape the remuneration. Secret retributions are always restoring the level, when disturbed, of the Divine justice. It is impossible to tilt the beam. All the tyrants and proprietors and monopolists of the world in vain set their shoulders to heave the bar. Settles for evermore the ponderous equator to its line, and man and mote and star and sun must range with it, or be pulverized by the recoil.[2]

The original source of this truth is the Great Commandments (Matthew 22:36-40). God has given us simple but crystal clear guidelines on how to live a happy and full life:

"Teacher, which is the greatest commandment in the Law?" Jesus replied: "'Love the Lord your God with all your heart and with all your soul and with all your mind'. This is the first and greatest commandment. And the second is like it: 'Love your neighbor as yourself.' All the Law and the Prophets hang on these two commandments."

So, sometimes we play a role in the situations we find ourselves in. This is the result of conscious decisions we make, driven by powerful biological and psychological needs arising from our fallen nature as human beings. Repeatedly making bad, selfish decisions will result in a difficult and painful life. There is no doubt about that. As noted above, though, a lot of things happen that are simply out of our control and make no logical sense – *based on what we can see and understand.*

What we can see and understand, though, is limited. We are not God, nor do we have God's full view that spans all of eternity. As my friend Ken Pargament once told me, quoting an old Balinese saying, "We are like water buffalo watching a symphony." Being limited in our view, we cannot fully understand and appreciate the symphony going on around us. God is the conductor, ensuring that every instrument is played in tune and on time. The melody being played includes pain and suffering. God has somehow even worked evil into the melody.

While we may be water buffaloes compared to God, I believe he usually speaks to us in ways we can understand. We were created as rational beings, and so God communicates to us through logic. Some traumatic events, though, truly defy logic. There is a promise in the scriptures that one day we will know and understand. That day may not be until after we've crossed over the river into eternity. Until then, our only option is to trust the one who loves us.

> *For now we see through a glass, darkly; but then face to face: now I know in part; but then shall I know even as also I am known* (1 Corinthians 13:12, KJV).

Life doesn't always make sense and isn't always fair. This fact, in my opinion, doesn't rule out the possibility that God is good, in control, and loves us more than any human has, will, or is even capable of. All the evil in the world today is not proof that God doesn't exist. No, Christians believe that it is proof that we need a savior and are simply unable – helpless on our own – to save ourselves. We may not be thieves, murders, or terrorists, but all of us "miss the mark" in one way or another through our greed, selfishness, and disregard for others. God is perfect and holy, and when we miss the mark, this prevents us from experiencing his presence and love.

In the Christian tradition, God's plans included a solution to the problem of evil. He would take care of it himself by appearing in person to save us from ourselves.

CHAPTER 7

Does God Love Christians?

§

I'VE BEEN USING THE WORD "Christian" liberally here. What exactly is a Christian? A Christian is someone who follows the teachings of Jesus Christ (i.e., Protestants, Catholics, Eastern Orthodox, etc.). While there are plenty of disagreements and controversies, most Christians agree on a set of statements set forth in the Nicene Creed (established at the first council of Nicaea in the 4th century, see Table at the end of this chapter).

Does God love Christians? We are told by Jesus in Matthew 18:3 that a person must become like a child to enter the kingdom of heaven. Therefore, Jesus might answer the question of whether God loves Christians in a way that even a child can understand: **a song**.

> *Jesus loves me! This I know,*
> *For the Bible tells me so;*
> *Little ones to Him belong;*
> *They are weak, but He is strong.*
> *Yes, Jesus loves me!*
> *Yes, Jesus loves me!*
> *Yes, Jesus loves me!*
> *The Bible tells me so.*[1]

Swiss theologian Karl Barth, called by Pope Pius XII "the most outstanding and consistently evangelical theologian that the world has seen in modern times" and "the most important theologian since Thomas Aquinas." While visiting the USA in 1962 lecturing at Princeton Theological Seminary and the University of Chicago, he was asked to summarize the central overriding message contained in his *Church Dogmatics* (consisting

---

1 Biography and hymns by Anna Bartlett Warner (1827-1915)

of 6 million words in 13 volumes). It is said that Barth thought for a moment and then exclaimed: "Jesus loves me, this I know, for the Bible tells me so."

The Bible says that God loves Christians. The Bible! Maybe the Bible is just a book of fairy tales. How reliable is this source called the Bible and what does it say about God's love for Christians?

The Bible

How many books have you read lately that were written thousands of years ago? There are only a handful of such books even in print today. None are science books. The first book of the Bible, likely Genesis or Job, was completed around 1400 BC. The most recent book of the Bible was written around 90 AD (Revelations). In other words, the Bible has been around for a long time.

According to Robert Darnton, the Carl H. Pforzheimer University Professor and Librarian Emeritus at Harvard, "Most books go out of print with astonishing rapidity. In fact, if they make it into bookstores (most don't), their shelf life is often a matter of days; and few of them continue to sell, even as e-books, after a year."[1] The average non-fiction U.S. book sells about 250 copies per year and less than 3000 copies over its lifetime. The average fiction U.S. book doesn't do much better. Publicist Steve Laube says: "If a novel sells 5,000 copies at one publisher they celebrate and have steak dinners." The top selling book (fiction and non-fiction) in modern times is "Tale of Two Cities" written in 1859 by Charles Dickens, which has sold 200 million copies to date. That is the **top** selling book.

The *Guinness Book of World Records* indicates that the Bible is the best-selling book of all time with over 5 **billion** copies sold and distributed since 1815. Over 100 million Bibles are sold or given away every year (according to *The Economist Magazine*). The Bible has been translated into 349 languages. Nearly 2500 languages (95% of the World's population) have at least one book of the

---

1 Darnton R. *The New York Review of Books*, 2011

Bible in their language. Does that say anything about the value of what is contained in this book?

GOD'S LOVE IN THE BIBLE

What does the best-selling book of all time say about God's love? Indeed, the Bible overflows with expressions of God's love. The New International Version of the Bible contains 551 mentions of the word "love." For Christians, the clearest evidence for God's love is John 3:16:

> *For God so loved the world that he gave his one and only Son, that whoever believes in him shall not perish but have eternal life.*

Christianity is based on the life, death, and resurrection of Jesus, who Christians call the Christ. This central event in history, Christians believe, was foretold by the prophet Isaiah nearly 800 years before it happened (Isaiah 53:3-5). The word for "Christ" in Hebrew is מָשִׁיחַ (*Māšîaḥ*) or the messiah ("anointed one").

In Jesus' time, the Jewish messiah was viewed as the person who would save or liberate the Jewish people. Many places in the Hebrew portion of the Bible and the Talmud (the central text of Rabbinic Judaism) foretell the coming of the messiah. Religious Jews today are still waiting for the messiah to come. The Jewish messiah is believed to be a human leader, physically descended from the line of King David. It is believed that the messiah will unify the tribes of Israel, gather all Jews to the land of Israel, rebuild the temple in Jerusalem, bring in a time of global peace, and announce the coming of heaven on earth (God's universal reign).

Christians believe that Jesus is the Jewish messiah and is Divine, i.e., that God appeared personally on earth as Jesus, taking on a human nature and experiencing all the feelings and longings that we feel. God chose to be vulnerable by coming into the world as a human being. He did so because he wanted to personally know and experience what his creatures were going through as a result of disobedience in the Garden. That includes the experience of horrific pain and suffering, and death itself.

Christians also believe that God by taking the form of a human in Jesus Christ did more than just experience what we experience. By his death and resurrection, Jesus actually reverses the fallen nature of humans that separates them by sin from a perfect and holy God. Jesus, who Christians believe never sinned, sacrificed himself so that every person who believes in him can stand sinless before God. Oswald Chambers emphasizes the importance of acknowledging and accepting Jesus' sacrifice:

> *It doesn't matter who or what we are, there is absolute reinstatement into God by the death of Jesus Christ, and by no other way, not because Jesus Christ pleads, but because He died. It is not earned, but accepted. All the pleading which deliberately refuses to recognize the Cross is of no avail; it is battering at another door than the one which Jesus has opened.* (ibid, December 8)

Thus, Christians believe that God himself paid the price for human sin by becoming a man and dying on the cross, making eternal life possible for every person who believes. God loves us so much that he himself came to make things right, something we could never do.

Notice that there is a phrase in John 3:16 that indicates who is eligible for this gift: "*whoever* believes in him." Christians believe that no matter who you are or what you've done, the "whoever" applies to you. If you've decided to believe in Jesus, the messiah, and what he has done for you, the gift is yours (say Christians, particularly conservative Protestants). The New Testament says that nothing can separate people from God's love, proven by his becoming a human, suffering and dying.

> *For I am convinced that neither death nor life, neither angels nor demons, neither the present nor the future, nor any powers, neither height nor depth, nor anything else in all creation,*

will be able to separate us from the love of God that is in Christ Jesus our Lord. (Romans 8:38-39)

This reinforces what was written long before:

Though the mountains be shaken and the hills be removed, yet my unfailing love for you will not be shaken nor my covenant of peace be removed," says the Lord, who has compassion on you. (Isaiah 54:10)

The New Testament says that God's love is like a father's love, which is how Jesus said people should refer to God when praying ("Our Father in heaven…" Matthew 6:9). The Jewish and Christian scriptures also say that God's love is like a mother's love (Isaiah 66:13), often using illustrations from nature (Deuteronomy 32:11; Matthew 23:37). Some of us, though, have not experienced the love of a father or a mother. The scriptures say that God loves us more than even the best father or best mother ever could:

Can a mother forget the baby at her breast and
have no compassion on the child she has borne?
Though she may forget, I will not forget you!
(Isaiah 49:15-16)

Although it's hard to imagine, Christians believe
that even their **enemies** are an example of God's
love. They believe that God will use their enemies
to form them into the people he desires. Goliath
made it possible for David to become the great
man and king that he later became. Joseph's brothers made it possible for him to go to Egypt and
become second in power only to the Pharaoh
himself, later saving his brothers and father from
starvation. It is our enemies that shape us into our
potential. Perhaps that is why Jesus said we should
love our enemies.

I believe that the sacred scriptures contain
two types of message. One message was written for the people of the day and depends heavily
on the situation or context during that historical
period. The second type of message was written for people of that day <u>and</u> for humanity more

generally, containing perennial truths that endure for all time. They were true at the beginning of time and will be true at the end of time. Perhaps this is why the scriptures have persisted for thousands of years. An example of one of those perennial truths is God's love.

Like the song goes, "Jesus loves me this I know for the Bible tells me so." Given how long the Bible has been around, and the fact that it continues to be the #1 best-selling book in the world, that sounds like pretty good evidence to me.

Besides Christians

Is there something special about Christianity that sets it apart from other world religions? Yes, there is something different about it. It is the only religion that claims God himself was born a human and then chose to die in order to cover sin, i.e., make up for people's mistakes so they can stand blameless before him some day. This seems ridiculous, even comical. But that is exactly what Christians believe about the magnitude of God's love.

But, is Christianity the only religion that emphasizes God's personal love according to its sacred scripture? What about Judaism (out of which Christianity emerged)? What does Judaism teach about God's love for Jews? What about Islam? Does the Qur'an claim that God loves Muslims? What about Hindus and Buddhists? As a scientist trying to examine the evidence, I'd like to know whether God loves people in these other faith traditions as well, or whether Christians are in some kind of exclusive club.

TABLE. THE NICENE CREED (325 AD, REVISED 381)

We believe in one God, the Father, the Almighty, maker of heaven and earth, of all that is seen and unseen.

We believe in one Lord, Jesus Christ, the only Son of God, eternally begotten of the Father, God from God, Light from Light, true God from true God, begotten, not made, one in Being with the Father.

Through him all things were made. For us men and for our salvation he came down from heaven: by the power of the Holy Spirit he was born of the Virgin Mary, and became man.

For our sake he was crucified under Pontius Pilate; he suffered, died, and was buried.

On the third day he rose again in fulfillment of the Scriptures; he ascended into heaven and is seated on the right hand of the Father.

He will come again in glory to judge the living and the dead, and his kingdom will have no end.

We believe in the Holy Spirit, the Lord, the giver of life, who proceeds from the Father and the Son. With the Father and the Son he is worshipped and glorified. He has spoken through the Prophets.

We believe in one holy catholic and apostolic Church.

We acknowledge one baptism for the forgiveness of sins.

We look for the resurrection of the dead, and the life of the world to come. Amen.

CHAPTER 8

Does God Love Jews?

∬

SOME MIGHT ARGUE that the emphasis in Judaism is placed more on people loving God, than on God loving people. Certainly, loving God is stressed:

Hear, O Israel: The HaShem our G-d, The HaShem is One. And thou shalt love HaShem thy G-d with all thy heart, and with all thy soul, and with all thy might. And these words, which I command thee this day, shall be upon thy heart; And thou shalt teach them diligently unto thy children, and shalt talk of them when thou sittest in thy house, and when thou walkest by the way, and when thou liest down, and when thou risest up. And thou shalt bind them for a sign upon thy hand, and they shall be for frontlets between thine eyes. And thou shalt write them upon the door-posts of thy house, and upon thy gates. (Devarim 6:4-9) (Deuteronomy)

While God commands Jews to love him, there is plenty of evidence from Jewish scripture (the Tanakh) that **the feelings are mutual**. Those scriptures indicate that the God of the Jews has emotions and feelings, and sometimes gets mad at his people. But, he also loves them deeply and hurts when they hurt.

For He said: 'Surely, they are My people, children that will not deal falsely'; so He was their Saviour. In all their affliction He was afflicted, and the angel of His presence saved them; in His love and in His pity He redeemed them; and He bore them, and carried them all the days of old. (Yisheyah 63:8-9) (Isaiah)

Consider the intensity of God's love:

> *For thou art a holy people unto HaShem thy G-d: HaShem thy G-d hath chosen thee to be His own treasure, out of all peoples that are upon the face of the earth. HaShem did not set His love upon you, nor choose you, because ye were more in number than any people--for ye were the fewest of all peoples-- but because HaShem loved you...* (Devarim 7:6-8) (Deuteronomy)

David Wolpe, named by Newsweek Magazine the most influential rabbi in America in 2012, examined God's love for Jews in the 2013 September 11th issue of *The Tablet* (a widely read American Jewish magazine). He begins with a description of the intimate relationship between God and Moses, and how this represents the love relationship between God and the Jewish people more generally. During Shema (the centerpiece of the morning and evening prayer services), Jews declare: "ahavat olam" (eternal love). The full statement is "With eternal

love, You have loved the house of Israel." Wolpe
describes it as a "love-saturated liturgy." He goes
on to say that God's love is "sewn into the fabric
of the universe" and that God created humans
because he was lonely, citing a collection of ancient
rabbinical homiletic interpretations of the book of
Numbers (*Bamidbar Rabbah* 13:6). The God of the
Jews desires to be close to his people and have a
relationship with them. In fact, God told Moses to
build him a tabernacle (Mishkan) so that he could
dwell right there with his people as they traveled
through the desert.

Are the Jewish people (and individual Jews)
God's beloved? Wolpe certainly thinks so. The
phrase "my beloved" is dōdi in Hebrew, and it
appears in the Judeo-Christian scriptures for the
first time in chapter 6, verse 3, of the Shir Hashirim
(Song of Solomon). In fact, lekha dōdi (לכה דודי) or
come my beloved is a passage in a Jewish song that
is recited at the synagogue on Friday just as the
sun sets to welcome the Sabbath prior to the evening service (part of the Kabbalat Shabbat ritual).
According to Wolpe, Jewish tradition holds that

the Song of Solomon expresses the love between God and Israel, an opinion shared by others as well (see Franz Rosenzweig's *Star of Redemption*, University of Wisconsin Press, 1970).

The Tanakh says that God loves the Jewish people, and will continue to love them forever.

> *Blessed be HaShem thy G-d, who delighted in thee, to set thee on the throne of Israel; because HaShem loved Israel forever, therefore made He thee king, to do justice and righteousness.* Melachim A 10:9 (1 Kings)

Also, consider the beautiful passage in Hosea that describes God's feelings for his beloved.

> *And I will betroth thee unto Me forever; yea, I will betroth thee unto Me in righteousness, and in justice, and in lovingkindness, and in compassion. And I will betroth thee unto Me in faithfulness; and thou shalt know HaShem.* (Hoshea 2:21-22)

Based on these verses, interpreted as God speaking to his people Israel, Wolpe says that: "The relationship between God and Israel is many things – a struggle, a tragedy, a triumph. But most of all, it is a love story. We are God's, and God is ours. Each morning, as the worshiper wraps tefillin around the middle finger, the betrothal verse from Hosea is recited…"

As in Christianity, God is portrayed in Jewish scriptures as one who cares and has compassion on his children like a loving parent (see Tehilim 103:13 and Yisheyah 66;13), yes, and above and beyond that.

> *For though my father and my mother have forsaken me, HaShem will take me up. Teach me Thy way, O HaShem; and lead me in an even path….* (Tehilim 27:10-11)

Few scriptures refer to God's steadfast love as eloquently as Tehilim 139: 7-12:

> *Whither shall I go from Thy spirit? or whither shall I flee from Thy presence?*

> *If I ascend up into heaven, Thou art there; if I make my bed in the nether-world, behold, Thou art there.*
>
> *If I take the wings of the morning, and dwell in the uttermost parts of the sea;*
>
> *Even there would Thy hand lead me, and Thy right hand would hold me.*
>
> *And if I say: 'Surely the darkness shall envelop me, and the light about me shall be night';*
>
> *Even the darkness is not too dark for Thee, but the night shineth as the day; the darkness is even as the light.*

Yes, there is plenty of evidence that God loves the Jewish people, not only as a people group but also as individuals. But there are conditions necessary to experience the love that is always present.

> *'Now therefore, if ye will hearken unto My voice indeed, and keep My covenant, then ye shall be Mine own treasure from among all peoples; for all the earth is Mine; and ye shall be unto Me*

*a kingdom of priests, and a holy nation. These
are the words which thou shalt speak unto the
children of Israel.'* (Shemot 19:5-6)

LAMENT

The chosen people were not a perfect people who
always followed God's advice. The Jewish scriptures are full of passages expressing lament and
pleas for mercy to a loving God, but also one who
is just and fair. Consider, King David, who saw
himself as God's favored son ("He shall call unto
Me - Thou art my Father, my G-d, and the rock of
my salvation" – see Tehilim 89:27). This son was
lustful and conniving, intentionally planning and
carrying out a murder. He must confess and plead
for mercy:

*Remember not the sins of my youth, nor
my transgressions; according to Thy mercy
remember Thou me, for Thy goodness' sake,
O HaShem.* (Tehilim 25:7; see also Tehilim
94:18)

David is repentant and admits that his sin is against God alone:

> *For I know my transgressions; and my sin is ever before me. Against Thee, Thee only, have I sinned, and done that which is evil in Thy sight; that Thou mayest be justified when Thou speakest, and be in the right when Thou judgest.* (Tehilim 51:5-6)

GOD'S RESPONSE

Despite David's serious mistakes, God answers his pleas for mercy and forgiveness because he loves those with a repentant heart.

> *I will be glad and rejoice in Thy lovingkindness; for Thou hast seen mine affliction, Thou hast taken cognizance of the troubles of my soul,* (Tehilim 31:8; see also Tehilim 103:4)

God's responses convince David that he is the beloved of God:

That Thy beloved may be delivered, save with Thy right hand, and answer me (Tehilim 108:7)

The New Testament describes God's feelings toward David as "a man after my own heart." Thus, just as David who committed terrible transgressions of the moral law, everyone who is repentant has the potential to be men and women after God's own heart.

But for many Jews…questions remain.

The Holocaust

God's love for the Jewish people may be difficult to reconcile with the Holocaust (for which there is no logical explanation or justification). However, God's response to Job during his time of suffering may help some Jews who have rejected God because they feel betrayed by the horror of what happened.

In Eyov 1:1, Job is described as a man who was "whole-hearted and upright, and one that feared

G-d, and shunned evil." He was a good man, a religious man who helped others both with his finances and his counsel. After everything was taken from Job, i.e., his family, children, his possessions, and health (similar to what many Jews in the concentration camps experienced), he asked why?

> *Why died I not from the womb? Why did I not perish at birth? Why did the knees receive me? And wherefore the breasts, that I should suck?... Why hast Thou set me as a mark for Thee, so that I am a burden to myself? And why dost Thou not pardon my transgression, and take away mine iniquity?* (Eyov 3:11-12, 7:20-21)

What was God's answer?

> *Then HaShem answered Job out of the whirlwind, and said: Who is this that darkeneth counsel by words without knowledge? ... Where wast thou when I laid the foundations of the*

earth? Declare, if thou hast the understanding.
Who determined the measures thereof, if thou
knowest? (Eyov 38:1-2, 4-5)

God is saying to Job that he just doesn't have all the
information necessary to fully understand what is
going on. It is indeed difficult to make sense of
what happened during the Holocaust. We may be
like water buffaloes listening to a symphony (chapter 4), but that lack of understanding is still painful
and confusing to many who lost loved ones. Yet
God insists, "You are my beloved."

CHAPTER 9

Does God Love Muslims?

§

THERE IS NO BETTER EVIDENCE of God's love for Muslims than the Qur'an. Christianity is based on the life, death, and resurrection of Jesus Christ. Islam (and the entire religious life of the Muslim) is based on the Qur'an. To Muslims, this is the greatest gift that God could possibly give.

The Qur'an is a holy book whose nature is different from that of the Judeo-Christian scriptures. Most Jews and Christians view their scriptures as having been written by humans, but inspired by God. Muslims believe that the author of the Qur'an is God himself. The Prophet Mohammad was not inspired by God. He was a vehicle through which God directly transmitted his words to humanity. In Islam, the Qur'an is the "word of God" like Jesus is the "word of God" in Christianity. The Qur'an has sold over 800 million copies, and is the most "recited" book in the world today (the word Qur'an in Arabic means "recitation" or "he recited").

The central theme of the Qur'an is the one-ness, greatness, and majesty of God, who in Islam is called Allah (الله). The word Allah is mentioned over 2,500 times in the Qur'an. In the Arab world today, this name for God is even included in many common greetings (e.g., "Ahlan sadiqi") and in response to those greetings (e.g., "Al-ḥamdu lillāh," "Ahlan wa sahlan," "inshallah").

Fazlur Rahman (1919-1988), one of the most esteemed Muslim theologians of the 20th century, said:

> *In discussing God…the idea of monotheism— which is logically imperative – is made the foundation stone of the entire treatment* [Qur'an],

and all other Qur'anic ideas on God are either derived from it or subsumed under it...[1]

The Qur'an repeatedly says that it is just a reminder -- a reminder of what is already known. According to Fazlur Rahman, the Qur'an sometimes calls itself (and sometimes calls the Prophet) "a reminder." What is it a reminder of? Rahman says:

(1) that everything except God is contingent on God, including the entirety of nature (which has a 'metaphysical' and a 'moral' aspect); (2) that God, with all His might and glory, is essentially the all-merciful God; and (3) that both these aspects necessarily entail a proper relationship between God and Man – a relationship of the served and the servant – and consequently also a proper relationship between man and man.

1 Rahman F (1980). *Major Themes of the Qur'an.* Chicago, IL: University of Chicago Press

God's Love in Islam

The Qur'an describes God as loving. It says *"wa huwa al-ghafour al-wadoud,"* i.e., "He is the Most Forgiving, the Most Loving" (85:15). Indeed, one of the names for God in the Qur'an is *al-Wadud* ("the one who loves" or "the loving one").

While the word "love" is not emphasized as much in Islam as in Christianity, a closely related word is used to describe *the primary characteristic* of God. The word is **mercy**. In fact, another name for God in the Qur'an is the word "al-Rahman" – which in Arabic means "the Merciful" or "the Compassionate." Thus, mercy is a key attribute of God in Islam. If you doubt this, note that the *first* verse (aya) of the Qur'an (1:1) says: "In the name of God, the Lord of Mercy, the Giver of Mercy!"[1] This verse is repeated at the start of every one of the 114 chapters contained in the Qur'an (the only exception is the 9th chapter). The complete verse in Arabic is "Bismi Allāhi Ar-Raĥmāni Ar-Raĥīmi"

---

1 Abdel Haleem MAS (translator) (2004). *The Qur'an*. NY, NY: Oxford World Classics, p 3 [all verses from the Qur'an quoted here are from this translation unless otherwise noted]

Harold G. Koenig, M.D.

(بِسْمِ اللهِ الرَّحْمنِ الرَّحِيمِ). It is also the phrase that begins every prayer (Salat) that Muslims say five times a day. Thus, God's mercy and compassion are a core theme of the Qur'an, second only to the oneness of God.

While much is said about God's wrath *(gha-dab)* in Islam, the use of that word is much less common in the Qur'an than are words describing his mercy and compassion. The *Jawshan al-Kabir* is a well-known Muslim prayer often said during Ramadan. The prayer contains 250 names for God and 750 attributes. Among the names for God is the one "whose mercy has preceded His wrath." Even God's wrath, though, is a sign that he cares and is concerned. God experiences negative emotions when people hurt themselves or hurt others. He wishes they would correct their behavior – which sometimes requires a few threats.

In Islam, as in Judaism, God's love is one reason for creation itself. In a widely known hadith (Hadith Qudsi), God says: "I was a hidden treasure; I loved to be known. Hence I created the world so that I would be known." Why would God need to

72

be known? Mahnaz Heydarpoor says "The purpose behind His love to be known is understandable by considering the fact that God who is the Wise, the Compassionate and the Omnipotent, creates the universe and particularly human beings to give them the maximum grace and perfection they have the capacity for receiving."[2] Thus, Muslims believe that God created humans in order to love them and allow them to experience his love.

Indeed, the God of Islam is not a distant God uninvolved with creation. The Qur'an says, "We created man and We know what the negative whisperings of his mind are and We are nearer to him than his jugular vein!" (50:16). The jugular vein was an important part of human anatomy in the Prophet Mohammad's time, since life depended on this large vein located close to the surface of the neck that could be easily severed during battle resulting in almost instant death. God is saying that he is closer to Muslims than life itself, knows everything, and wants to be involved in everything.

---

2 Heydarpoor M (2001). Divine Love: Love as the highest reason for creation (http://www.al-islam.org).

EXPERIENCE OF GOD'S LOVE IS CONDITIONAL

As in Christianity and Judaism, the ability to experience God's love in Islam depends on a person's actions. Some experience God's love and favor more than others. Bad actions can prevent the experience of God's love, which is always there.

> *You who believe, if any of you go back on your faith, God will soon replace you with people He loves and who love Him, people who are humble towards the believers, hard on the disbelievers, and who strive in God's way without fearing anyone's reproach. Such is God's favour.* (5:54)

The Qur'an is clear on who will experience God's love: the just and fair (3:56, 3:140, 4:107, 5:42, 49:9, 60:8), those who keep their word and think about God (3:76, 9:4, 9:7), those who do good (2:195, 3:134; 3:148, 5:13, 5:93, 7:55-56), those who are humble (4:36), those who do not give up during hard times (3:146), those who repent of their sins and keep themselves pure (2:222), those who put their trust in God (3:159), those who are grateful (2:276), and those who fight for God's cause (61:4).

Thus, God's love is available to all, but the experience of that love depends on a person's ACTIONS. Admitting one's errors, repenting of them, and deciding to surrender to God and live according to his rules – enables a Muslim to experience God's love:

> *Say, '[God says], My servants who have harmed yourselves by your own excess, do not despair of God's mercy. God forgives all sins: He is truly the Most Forgiving, the Most Merciful* (39:53; see also 2:222 and 24:22)

Although Muslims believe that on the Last Day good deeds and evil deeds will be weighed, and the person will suffer the consequences of their actions in the hereafter (7:8-9; 101:6-11), a good deed weighs a lot more than a bad deed according to the Qur'an:

Whoever has done a good deed will have it ten times to his credit, but whoever has done a bad deed will be repaid only with its equivalent (6:160).

Muslims believe in a Last Day, and on that Day there is judgement. Because God is perfectly holy, he cannot excuse sin and cannot allow humans who are driven by their sinful nature to enter paradise with him. Paradise with God is only for those who are good (or whose good deeds outweigh their bad deeds). Some Muslims feel fear and anxiety over these beliefs. However, instilling fear appears to be God's last resort. Muslims believe that because God loves us, he welcomes with open arms those who turn to him. Judgement is accompanied by tremendous mercy and compassion, and a negative judgment is done only with the greatest sorrow. Yes, God judges, but he desperately wants to acquit us.

The Qur'an says…"those who have attained to faith love God more than all else" (2:165). For the Muslim who loves God, then, the fear of judgement day will disappear. Those who love God will not want to disobey him or harm those he loves. Serving God out of love for him is a lot better than serving out of fear. **You can't fear someone you love.** The Qur'an says, "Why should God make you suffer torment if you are thankful and believe in Him? God always rewards gratitude…" (4:147). Some say that serving God because of love (rather than fear) is one of the highest forms of worship a Muslim can engage in and is the highest spiritual level that can be achieved.[1]

Living on one's own terms, making one's own decisions, and following one's own desires and pleasures may impede the experience of God's love (as it does in Christianity and Judaism). In contrast, placing God first, seeking justice, and caring for those unable to care for themselves -- this removes all barriers to God's love.

---

1 Green K (2015). Love for God in Islam: The highest attribute of spiritual attainment. *IslamiCity*, March 15

CHAPTER 10

Does God Love Buddhists?

§

WHAT ABOUT BUDDHISTS? Does God love those who may not even believe he exists (or is personal)? The following is what I could find on beliefs about God and God's love in the Pali Cannon, the sacred scripture of Buddhism.

I am not very familiar with Buddhism, and so admit to being an amateur in saying anything about what Buddhists believe, including beliefs about God's love for them. According to what I could find (confirmed by Buddhist experts who I consulted), belief in a personal God or a creator God is not a teaching of the Buddha in the Pali Cannon (an oral tradition from the 5th/4th century

BC that was written down around the 1st century BC). When asked his opinion about a Supreme Being, the Buddha reportedly either remained silent or discouraged such questions. He wanted his followers to focus on virtuous goals and compassion, rather than be distracted by theological speculations about God or gods that were common among religious scholars of his time. Therefore, while the Buddha taught that we should focus on righteous living and virtuous actions, belief in a personal God who loves people (or whom people should love and worship) was not something the Buddha taught. However, the Buddha never explicitly ruled out the existence of God either.

Much less clear, however, is what the Buddha's followers actually thought of **him** after his death (or how Buddhists today more generally consider him). Do some Buddhists love and worship the Buddha as non-Buddhists worship God? Most Buddhist authorities say that Buddhists do not pray to or worship the Buddha as God, but rather emphasize that such activities are gestures of respect and admiration for the Buddha and his teachings. Very shortly after his death, however, devotees started to build relics of the Buddha to worship and it became customary to make pilgrimages to places where he had walked. As Buddhism spread to various places in the East, a number of cultures included a devotional element to Buddhism (e.g., Mahayana Buddhism, Pure Land Buddhism, etc.). According to Encyclopedia Britannica:

> *While the contemplative elite may deny the real existence of gods and demons together with the rest of phenomenal existence, the majority of Buddhists from the earliest times in India, and in other countries where Buddhism has spread, have never neglected indigenous religious beliefs.*[1]

There is no specific "sutta" (discourse of the Buddha) in the Pali Cannon where the Buddha asks his

---

1 Buddhism. *Encyclopedia Britannica*. Encyclopedia Britannica Premium Service, 2004

disciples to love or seek help from him as a divine being. Nevertheless, he does advise his disciples to <u>take refuge</u> in the Triple Gem ("triratna"), which is known as the central focus of inspiration and devotion in Buddhism. The Triple Gem are (1) Buddha (the enlightened one), (2) Dhamma (Buddha's teachings or eternal truth), and (3) Sangha (the community of disciples who are at some stage of Awakening). In fact, when converting to Buddhism, one will often say, "I take refuge in the Buddha. I take refuge in the Dharma. I take refuge in the Sangha."

> *He who has gone for refuge to the Buddha, the Teaching and his Order, penetrates with transcendental wisdom the Four Noble Truths — suffering, the cause of suffering, the cessation of suffering, and the Noble Eightfold Path leading to the cessation of suffering.* (Dhammapada, verse 190-191, part of the Pali Cannon)

Therefore, the Buddha may or may not be viewed by his followers as God, depending on the particular culture in which it is practiced.

Many Buddhists, then, seek good luck and protection from the Buddha, his disciples, and divine beings. This is true for both Theravada and Mahayana Buddhists, but as noted above, especially the latter. For example, in Mahayana Buddhism (widespread in China, Tibet, Japan, and Korea), there is belief in bodhisattvas or compassionate beings that exist in the highest level of heaven and serve to guard the world and work to alleviate suffering. Mahayana Buddhists consider the Buddha to be an embodiment of the cosmic Dharmakāya, which has been described in Wikipedia as "the unmanifested, 'inconceivable' (*acintya*) aspect of Buddha, out of which Buddhas arise and to which they return after their dissolution." As a novice here, that description sounds a lot like God to me.

In addition, some Mahayana Buddhists worship Avalokiteśvara ("Lord who looks down," translated from Sanskrit). Avalokiteśvara is a bodhisattva who embodies mercy, compassion, kindness and love, a divine being who appears to have some of the characteristics of a loving personal God. One of the most powerful and influential of the Mahayana sutras is the Lotus Sutra. Consider the following section from chapter 25 in the Lotus Sutra titled "The Universal Door of Gwan Shr Yin Bodhisattva." Gwan Shr Yin (whose name is translated 'the bodhisattva who contemplates the sounds or cries of the human world') is another name for the Avalokitesvara bodhisattva.

At that time Inexhaustible Intention Bodhisattva rose from his seat, uncovered his right shoulder, placed his palms together, and facing the Buddha, said, "World Honored One, by means of what causes and conditions is the Bodhisattva Gwan Shr Yin called 'Gwan Shr Yin'?"

The Buddha told Inexhaustible Intention Bodhisattva, "Good Man, if any of the limitless hundreds of thousands of myriads of kotis of living beings who are undergoing all kinds of suffering hear of Gwan Shr Yin Bodhisattva and recite his name single-mindedly, Gwan Shr Yin Bodhisattva will immediately hear their voices and rescue them.

If a person who upholds the name of Gwan Shr Yin Bodhisattva enters a great fire, the fire will not burn him, all because of this Bodhisattva's awesome spiritual power.

If a person being tossed about in the great sea calls out the Bodhisattva's name, he will find a shallow place.

If the hundreds of thousands of myriads of kotisof beings who seek gold, silver, lapis lazuli, mother-of-pearl, carnelian, coral, amber, real pearls, and so forth enter the great sea, an evil wind may toss their boats into the territory of the rakshasha ghosts. But if among them there is even one person who calls out the name of Gwan Shr Yin Bodhisattva, they will all be saved from the difficulty of the rakshashas.

For this reason, he is called Gwan Shr Yin.[1]

---

1 The Wonderful Dharma Lotus Flower Sutra Chapter Twenty-five, "The Universal Door of Gwan Shr Yin Bodhisattva" (http://www.cttbusa.org/dfs25/dfs25.asp)

Thus, there are a number of different beliefs in Buddhism (as there are in Christianity, Judaism, and Islam). As a result, generalizations are difficult to make. Nevertheless, many Buddhists believe in a divine being, one who is deeply compassionate and responds to human need.

CHAPTER 11

Does God Love Hindus?

〰

HINDUISM, OUT OF WHICH BUDDHISM arose, includes teachings about a personal God whom individuals can love and worship. The sacred scriptures of Hindus are the Vedas, the Upanishads (last section of the Vedas), and most relevant to our topic here, the Bhagavad Gita. Some Hindus believe that God does not have any specific attributes or form. *NriguNa brahman* is the name given to this aspect of God. Without attribute or form, a personal relationship with God is not possible. However, there is also belief in God who takes a personal form that has good attributes (*SaguNa brahman*). Hinduism, then, supports the worship of either a formless God or a God who has attributes, both of whom are understood as the same God. Hindus can relate to the personal aspect of God who has attributes such as strength and power, and who is good. In Hinduism, the Supreme God (Brahman) is manifested in three forms as Brahma (the creator), Vishnu (the preserver), and Shiva (the transformer).

According to Mariasusai Dhavamony, there are teachings of Divine grace and Divine love in the Upanishads.[1] However, it is the Bhagavad Gita that "introduces a new dimension of love of God for people and [love of] people for God." In the Bhagavad Gita (literally, "Song of the Lord"), Lord Krishna is presented as the eighth avatar – the incarnation or manifestation of the Supreme God Brahman who descends to earth. He is said to engage in relationships with those who are devout believers in him. This includes saving individuals from the effects of their own actions and karma:

---

1 Dhavamony M (2002). *Hindu-Christian Dialogue: Theological Soundings and Perspectives*. Amsterdam, Netherlands: Rodopi Bv Editions

> *Even if one committing the most abominable
> actions renders service only unto Me exclu-
> sively without deviation; one is to be consid-
> ered saintly because one is correctly resolved
> and properly situated. One swiftly becomes
> endowed with righteousness and justly obtains
> everlasting peace. O Arjuna declare it boldly,
> My devotee never perishes.* (Bhagavad Gita
> 9:30-31)[2]

The Bhagavad Gita, written down somewhere
between 600 BC and 200 AD, is a dialogue between
the Pandava prince Arjuna and Lord Krishna who
guides him. Arjuna has the duty to fight in the
righteous war between the Pandavas and Kauravas.
Lord Krishna instructs Arjuna to fight as a warrior
to establish Dharma (duties, rights, laws, conduct,
virtues and 'right way of living'). In the following verses of the Bhagavad Gita, Lord Krishna
explains to Arjuna who is dear to him:

---

2 *Bhagavad Gita* (http://www.bhagavad-gita.org/Gita/chap-
ter-12.html)

That devotee of Mine who is non-envious possessing benevolence towards all living entities, compassionate with no sense of proprietorship; free from false ego, equal in distress and happiness, forgiving, the always content one perfecting the science of uniting the individual consciousness with the Ultimate Consciousness, self-controlled, with unflinching determination, dedicating mind and spiritual intelligence upon me is very dear to Me.

One from whom any person is never disturbed and one who is never disturbed from any person and who is freed from the mundane pleasures, anger, fear and anxiety, such a one is very dear to Me.

That devotee of Mine who is desire-less, pure, expert, free from worry, free from agitation, unconcerned with any mundane endeavor, such a one is very dear to me.

One who rejoices not, dislikes not, grieves not, and desires not, impartial to both what is auspicious and inauspicious engaged in devotional service, such a one is very dear to Me.

That person who is equal to an enemy as well as a friend, also in honor and dishonor, impartial in cold, heat, happiness and distress, exempt from attachment, equipoised in praise or repute, contemplative before speaking, satisfied with whatever comes on its own accord, not attached to domestic life, fixed in determination and engaged in devotional service; such a one is very dear to Me.

Endowed with resolute faith in devotion to Me, those who worship this nectarian path of righteousness as described; these devotees are very, very dear to me. (Bhagavad Gita 12: 13-20)

Elsewhere, near the end of the Gita, Lord Krishna says:

Just think of Me, be My devotee, worship Me, offer obeisances unto Me, certainly you will come to Me, I promise this in truth to you being dear to Me. (Bhagavad Gita 18:65)

Dhavamony notes that the Bhagavad Gita emphasizes that while good action and right living "paves the way to liberation, it is [through] God's grace alone that one attains the liberated state and enters into union with him in love and bliss" (p 88). Thus, Hindus believe that the Supreme God cares enough to descend to earth, and is personified as a divine being characterized by grace and love. But, as in sacred scriptures from other faith traditions, the experience of God's love in Hinduism is based on our actions (with deep elements of grace).

CHAPTER 12

Does God Love Veterans?

§

Let's now consider a specific group of people not related to a particular faith tradition. I focus here on Veterans and active duty Service Members who may be dealing with inner conflict resulting from their experiences during war. Although my father and my father-in-law were both combat Veterans in World War II, I don't have much personal experience here. I served a very short stint in the Army, but was never deployed. My greatest stress was during boot camp when I discovered my bunkmate was regularly urinating in my boots at night, not wishing to walk the long distance from the barracks to the latrine.

Not everyone experiences psychological or physical wounds while serving their country. Most feel that they did the job they were asked to do, and are proud they could serve a role in protecting our country and the free world. But, a sizeable minority did become wounded (physically or psychologically), including some that developed post-traumatic stress disorder or PTSD. Because of the trauma that military personnel often experience during war, the resulting emotions may prevent or make it difficult to feel God's love. Some believe that God couldn't possibly love them after what happened. Some feel obligated and determined to pay for their actions for the rest of their lives.

It's difficult to experience God's love when you're carrying around a burden of guilt, shame or anger because of what you did (or did not do) out there on the battlefield. In the words of Jonathan Shay, some military personnel feel that they have "betrayed what is right in a high stakes situation." Not only betrayed what is right, but they themselves feel betrayed for being placed in situations where they had no other choice but to do what they did. Sometimes forced, sometimes willingly, these men and women may have done inhumane things to the enemy during wartime. Now, some cannot get those images out of their mind, images that come back in the form of flashbacks or horrific nightmares that haunt and disrupt both day and night.

How do you experience God's love when you don't think you deserve it? How do you experience God's love when you are in the throes of depression or severe anxiety, barely able to function, or are imprisoned by drugs or alcohol due to unsuccessful attempts to bury these experiences or numb the painful emotions that accompany them? What if your spouse left you or your children won't speak to you because you just can't relate to anybody now? What about a thousand other experiences during and after war that may be blocking your ability to receive or give love to those around you? If you are a Veteran or active duty Service Member who experienced emotional or spiritual wounds while serving your country, are you doomed to feel this way forever?

If you think that, then consider some of the great religious figures in the Bible, the Qur'an, and the Bhagavad Gita. Many of these religious leaders were military personnel who fought in wars to preserve their way of life or faith tradition. Not all acted in ways that were honorable. They were distressed by these experiences and often regretted what they did during combat. Here are just a few of them. There was Arjuna in the Bhagavad Gita who was hesitant to fight in the righteous war between Pandavas and Kauravas, requiring that Lord Krishnan (God) strongly encourage him to do so. There was Moses in the Bible who killed an Egyptian and ran away. There was Joshua who led the Jewish armies, but suffered defeat more than one time for failure to follow God's directions. There was David, the author of the Psalms, written when he was fleeing from Saul who was trying to kill him. He messed up many times both before and after he became king. The same was true for the Prophet Mohammad, who participated in numerous wars as he was establishing monotheistic Islam in a polytheistic Bedouin culture. There were many times when he struggled with doubt, fatigue and failure.

Jesus himself was betrayed by some of his closest friends. He fought for his life as he was brutally beaten and nailed to a cross. During this time of agonizing pain, he felt forsaken and deserted by God. Yet, it was to Jesus that God had said earlier, "You are my beloved" (Mark 1:11). In more recent times, there was Francis of Assisi, the founder of the Franciscan order of Catholic priests. He had previously been a soldier, was captured as a prisoner of war, and suffered from severe PTSD.

Take your pick. There are plenty of religious figures with whom those in the military can identify. They struggled with exactly the same moral and ethical dilemmas – fear, guilt, and shame, failure, betrayed by others, and abandoned by God.

If you are a Veteran who has recovered from the physical wounds of war, you may still be left with inner emotional conflicts that linger and resist healing. Psychologist Brett Litz says that those inner conflicts are often the result of a broken moral compass. When that happens, the way forward becomes dark and unclear. That darkness may lead to addiction or suicide in a desperate attempt to stop the confusion and pain. Even if the Veteran gets through the darkness initially, he (or she) is still at risk for re-experiencing symptoms later in life. PTSD symptoms often re-emerge when an older Veteran becomes physically ill and is no longer able to block out those memories by staying busy with work or other activity.

If you are a Veteran and have symptoms such as difficulty sleeping, nightmares or flashbacks, loss of interest, feeling numb, angry or irritable, or having recurring memories of traumatic war time experiences, this could be a sign you have PTSD. If so, it means you need treatment. That treatment includes attention to the "moral injury" that often accompanies PTSD and can block the healing process. [Note: some Veterans and active duty Service Members are offended by the term moral injury. It implies that they did something immoral while fighting the enemy, when in fact they were simply doing their job and following orders from their superiors. For that reason, we prefer to use the term "inner conflict" rather than moral injury.]

I have come to wonder if PTSD is at least partly the result of a *fractured relationship with God*. The experience of inconceivable horror can do that. The fracture in this relationship needs to be "reset" before most Veterans with this condition can really be whole again. You cannot erase the traumatic memories that come from wartime experiences that have become seared into your brain. However, you can lay down new neural pathways, which will allow the old pathways to atrophy. That's exactly what I'm talking about in this book: ways to lay down new neural pathways. The experience of God's love can transform and heal, leading to new purpose in life and re-engagement with others.

One way to begin is to visualize God (or Jesus, if you are Christian) gently touching you as an expression of his love for you. This is not just empty fantasy, but can actually help you come into contact with God's love, which is very real and very present. Remember Michelangelo's painting on the ceiling of the Sistine Chapel (chapter 4)? Look at it again. God is straining to touch the man. Recall also the parable of the leper in the New Testament. Many Veterans and active duty Service Members with PTSD feel like lepers. They feel different, separate from, untouchable by friends, family, or the sea of humanity around them. If you are a Veteran and feel that way, God wants to touch you and make you clean.

> *And there came a leper to him, beseeching him, and kneeling down to him, and saying unto him, if thou wilt, thou canst make me clean. And Jesus, moved with compassion, put forth his hand, and touched him, and saith unto him, I will; be thou clean.* (Mark 1:40-41, KJV)

In the Gospel of Luke, it says:

> *And he said unto him, Arise, go thy way: thy faith hath made thee whole.* (17:19, KJV)

For the Christian, the process of healing begins with Jesus' touch, which heals the fractured relationship with God and makes those who are wounded – physically, emotionally, and spiritually -- whole again. Indeed, we are all wounded to some degree and need outside help to be saved from ourselves and become whole. God's love can restore the wounded Veteran to a healthy and whole state, maybe even for the first time.

If you are a wounded warrior, you may think that God cannot possibly forgive you for what you did during wartime, or that you cannot forgive yourself. I believe that God loves you just the way you are right now. He loves the person **you see yourself to be** and wants to transform you so you can, as the old Army slogan goes, "be all you can be."

For Christians, the Bible says: "…God demonstrates his own love for us in this: While we were still sinners, Christ died for us" (Romans 5:8). God's love, if a person can accept and open up to it, will help them become the person they can't become on their own. If you are a wounded warrior (from war or simply from the hard battles of life) God wants you to become the person he knows you can be, and wants you to start now. Ecclesiastes 3:1-4 says there is a time for everything:

> *There is a time for everything, and a season for*
> *every activity under the heavens:*
> *a time to be born and a time to die,*
> *a time to plant and a time to uproot,*
> *a time to kill and a time to heal,*
> *a time to tear down and a time to build,*
> *a time to weep and a time to laugh,*
> *a time to mourn and **a time to dance**...*

It's time to heal, whether you are 20, 50, 75 or 95 years old. If you feel like you are drowning in waters of despair, then grasp God's outstretched hand and hold on. There will *come a time to dance.*

CHAPTER 13

How does God Love Us?

§

THE CENTRAL MESSAGE that God loves us is consistent across all major faith traditions. It is also true for a specific group of individuals who serve or served in the armed forces to preserve the freedom of people around the world, including the freedom to practice religion (*and the freedom not to*).

So, exactly how does God love us? Without knowing that, we might miss it. God loves us in many ways – some that we are aware of and some that we are not. Here are 10 of them, and these are not the only ones.

THE FREEDOM TO CHOOSE

As indicated in chapter 5, the freedom to choose is what makes us truly human and separates us from the rest of the animal kingdom and everything else in the universe that simply follows the laws of nature. We are unique in that regard and are like God in this respect, able to participate in creation itself. We are not required to believe in God, love him or follow his rules. We can choose not to. Giving us that option expresses how much God loves us. It literally makes love possible.

PEOPLE

God loves us by putting people in our lives that can have a positive influence on us, i.e., can help to shape and form us into the person God intends. Those people may not always be our best friends. They are often not like us. They may not support or encourage us in the way we are now. They are not usually the family members who naturally love us. They are not those whom we naturally love or are drawn to. They certainly can be, but usually are not. No, instead they are the irritating spouse, the wayward child, the unpleasant co-worker, or the nasty boss. It is in relating to people that are demanding or different from us that God shapes us, sometimes hammers us into our potential.

The Big Things

God sometimes gives us what we want: a great job becomes available, an unexpected check arrives, a baby is born without complications, an illness is healed, a relationship is mended, and many other good things that we hope and pray for. It is easy to think that God loves us only when we get what we want or something good happens. That view is too limited. If you have children, think of what you do for them – the things you provide them, the protection and attention. You want to help and guide them. Do you always give them what they want? Of course not. You give them what they *need*, including experiences that will help them develop into successful adults.

Harold G. Koenig, M.D.

THE LITTLE THINGS

God shows us the depth of his love by the little things. This is when he gives us grace and blesses us even when we don't deserve it. God is so generous, sometimes in large ways but more often in small ways that are easily missed. The parking space that suddenly opens up; the plane or bus that is delayed when we are running late; the unexpected call from a friend; a nice holiday spent with family; a considerate person who lets us in line at the store or on the road; a good meal; a great movie; and on and on it goes. Acknowledging the many small blessings from God and expressing thanks is one way to experience God's love on a regular basis.

ABILITIES AND TALENTS

God loves us by giving us special talents and abilities. Those talents may be natural or learned. Examples of talents include physical or athletic abilities, musical talents, ability to teach, lead, or administrate, ability to write, ability to provide financial assistance, desire to help others, show compassion, be merciful, encourage, or simply listen to others, and many more. Such abilities will often bring us joy, peace, purpose, and fulfillment. For these talents to result in that, however, they have to be "housed" in character. In other words, they must be used within a framework of moral and ethical values that guide, direct, and sometimes limit them. Abilities and talents can be used for destructive or self-serving purposes just as they can be used for God. They are usually accompanied by a sense of God's love and power when used for him.

GUIDELINES

God loves us by providing guidelines on how to live life to the fullest. These are the laws that he has established that run both the external physical universe and the internal universe of our minds. They include the moral laws, values, and ethical standards that if followed will help us to avoid the pain and suffering that will invariably plague us if we live by our own rules.

SPEAKS TO US

God speaks to us in that small quiet voice through our conscience, guiding our steps to help us to be safe, useful and productive. That voice is never condemning or harsh. It is usually a loving, barely audible voice that nudges, encourages, and sometimes carries us when the going gets rough.

IS AVAILABLE

God loves us by being available 24-7, every moment of the day and night, ready to respond to our call. God is only a thought away. He's never too busy. This is one of the least recognized ways that God shows he cares. There is no place that we don't have immediate access to God if we desire it. Nothing can separate us from God or from God's love for us. This is what both the Jewish (Psalm 139:1-18) and the Christian (Romans 8:39) scriptures promise.

THE HOLY SCRIPTURES

God loves us by giving us the Holy Scriptures – the Bible, the Qur'an, the Bhagavad Gita, the Pali Canon, and the writings of holy men and women in other faith traditions (including the humanist tradition). These writings provide us with important truths, teach us lessons, and provide examples of people who have gone through hard times and triumphed. They teach us to be humble and to realize that we cannot make it on our own, nor do we have to. They include inspirational writings by his servants like Henri Nouwen that remind us that we are God's beloved.

DIFFICULT EXPERIENCES

This way of loving us requires a bit more explanation (remember chapter 5?). God shows his love by allowing us to encounter difficult circumstances. Sometimes we've put ourselves in those situations because of poor choices. At other times, we are there simply because bad things happen in a fallen world like ours. These situations can make us angry, frustrated, and cause us to question God and push him away. But, they can also force us along a spiritual path that ends in a deeper experience with God that ultimately makes us complete and whole. But why use adversity and pain to do that? As I said before, most of us are not willing to change until we encounter experiences that involve tragedy or loss, until something upsets our lives and makes us ready to move on. When things are going well, in contrast, we fight to maintain the status quo and keep things exactly as they are. Spiritual advancement occurs only when pain forces us to grow.

Allowing bad things to happen in our lives and using them to produce growth, then, is one way that God loves us. Remember, I'm not saying that if your best friend was killed and dismembered right in front of you, or if you were forced into a situation where you had to kill a child or mother, or if your only daughter is raped and killed or maimed for life -- that God orchestrated these events in order to cause pain to help you grow. Some things happen that grieve God as much if not more than they grieve us. These situations do not result from God's will. Instead, they result from the decisions of deranged, lost individuals who God also grieves over, since they are his children too.

When things happen like this, I believe that God can turn the situation around for the victim and somehow protect them from the full weight of the experience. Perhaps that is wishful thinking. Nevertheless, there is wiring in the brain which makes this possible. When experiences become too intense, we automatically dissociate from the experience or retreat to a different place in our minds that blocks out the experience. We may even lose consciousness. There could also be other explanations about the way the universe is constructed that we cannot comprehend based on our limited knowledge and anchor in space and time -- all part of the incomprehensible symphony that God is orchestrating.

Although it is certainly a leap of faith, I believe that everything will be set right, if not in this life then in the life to come (Deuteronomy 32:4).

None of us know what the future holds or what lies beyond the grave, either for ourselves or our loved ones. Science certainly cannot tell us, nor will science ever be able to do so. All we know is what God has promised in his sacred scriptures – it is a promise that people of faith for thousands of years have clung to. For Christians, that promise is: "All things work together for good to them that love God, to them who are called according to his purpose" (Romans 8:28). I believe that God has a purpose and we are all being called to it, including those who are from other faith traditions or no faith tradition.

Begin to notice the many ways that God loves you. It will help you experience more of God's love, whether you feel it now or not.

CHAPTER 14

I don't feel God's Love

§

THERE ARE REASONS WHY YOU might not be able to feel God's love, even though it is constantly present and available. Here are some of the most common ones.

PAIN AND SUFFERING

When you are in the midst of difficult circumstances and are overwhelmed by feelings of anxiety, fear, disappointment, sadness or hurt, it can be hard -- if not impossible -- to feel God's love. God's love is there, but the pain blocks it out. The

Psalmist (King David) felt this way many times when things weren't going his way.

> *Look and see, there is no one at my right hand; no one is concerned for me. I have no refuge; no one cares for my life.* (Psalm 142:4; see also Psalm 22:1 and Psalm 77:8)

The same was true for Job, Jeremiah and other prophets, even Jesus.

> *And now my life ebbs away; days of suffering grip me. Night pierces my bones; my gnawing pains never rest.* (Job 30:16-17; see also Jeremiah 15:18 and Jeremiah 45:3)

> *The Lord is like an enemy; he has swallowed up Israel. He has swallowed up all her palaces and destroyed her strongholds. He has multiplied mourning and lamentation for Daughter Judah* (Lamentations 2:5)

And about the ninth hour Jesus cried with a loud voice, saying, Eli, Eli, lama sabachthani? That is to say, My God, my God, why hast thou forsaken me? (Matthew 27:46; see also Mark 15:34)

You are not alone in feeling forsaken, as if God's love has vanished or he is your enemy seeking to destroy you. Many in the Bible felt that way at one time or another – often just before some of their greatest accomplishments.

In the midst of these trials, in the absence of feeling God's love, all you can do is remember that it's there – God hasn't gone anywhere and doesn't feel any different about you, even while you are raging against him. If you don't give up or become settled in feeling resentful or angry at God, the feelings of his presence and love will eventually return as you get more distant from the painful event <u>and</u> continue to connect with him (even if the dialogue is a heated one).

IDOLATRY

I think God has a bit of a jealous streak in him.
He wants us to be loyal to him and him alone.
The Jewish scriptures and Qur'an are full of
verses that warn us not to worship anything other
than him. One king after another in Israel was
replaced because they would not take down the
"high places" where idol worship took place (e.g.,
Numbers 33:52, Leviticus 26:30). Whenever we
value something above God – things, people, ourselves (pride), lack of forgiveness – it will be difficult to experience God's love.

PERSECUTIONS

Persecutions will occur even if you have surrendered your life to God and are serving him faith-
fully. Jesus promised that to Christians:

> *"Truly I tell you," Jesus replied, "no one who*
> *has left home or brothers or sisters or mother or*
> *father or children or fields for me and the gospel*

*will fail to receive a hundred times as much in
this present age: homes, brothers, sisters, moth-
ers, children and fields—**along with persecutions**—and in the age to come eternal life.*
(Mark 10:29-30)

The same is true for Muslims. Sa'd ibn Abi
Waqqaas was a close companion of the Prophet
Mohammad and the leader of the Muslim army
that conquered Persia in 636 AD. According to a
hadith collected by Al-Tirmidhi, Abi Waqqaas is
said to have asked the Prophet:

*"O Messenger of Allah, which of the people are
most sorely tested?" He said: "The Prophets,
then the next best and the next best. A man will
be tested in accordance with his level of religious
commitment. If his religious commitment is
strong, he will be tested more severely, and if
his religious commitment is weak, he will be
tested in accordance with his religious commitment."* (al-Silsilah al-Saheehah, 143)

Thus, while much is gained by centering life on God, persecutions will occur as a result of the fallen nature of humanity and the cosmos, and the free choices that people make. When you are feeling persecuted, it is more difficult to feel God's love.

Past Traumas

A traumatic event from the past may be affecting your ability to experience God's love. While those difficult experiences can serve as a portal to a new and better life, they can also destroy mental and physical health. If the trauma is severe enough and the wound is still raw, it may be difficult to feel love from anybody, give love to anybody, or even love yourself. Post-traumatic stress disorder is a condition like that. As I mentioned in chapter 12, PTSD has devastating effects on a person's self-esteem, ability to trust others, and ability to form and maintain close relationships. You don't have to be a Veteran or in the military for that to occur.

CHILDHOOD EXPERIENCES

Another reason for not being able to feel God's love may go back to childhood. "Attachment theory" claims that there are four kinds of emotional attachment (including attachment to God) that result from experiences during this time. Those four kinds are: secure, ambivalent, avoidant, and disorganized. The last three are categorized as "insecure" forms (thought to make up about 30% of the general population).

The first form of attachment, s*ecure* attachment, is the healthiest. This develops when relationships with caregivers (mother and/or father) are consistent, predictable, and repairable. By repairable, I mean that when the relationship is disturbed for any reason, love and forgiveness quickly re-establish it.

The second form is *ambivalent* attachment. This develops when caregivers neglect a child, and then overindulge him or her to make up for the neglect. The experience of this back and forth kind of treatment confuses the child and interferes with the development of trust because they don't know what to expect from those caring for them.

The third form of attachment is *avoidant*. This develops when caregivers consistently neglect a child. Avoidant attachment occurs when the caregiver is emotionally unavailable to the child or is unresponsive to their needs, especially when the child is hurt or sick. Often not wanting to "spoil" the child, caregivers limit their affection or attention. They often discourage crying and force the child to be independent before the child is ready. As adults, such individuals rely heavily on self-soothing behaviors to cope with feelings of rejection and other negative emotions. Self-soothing behaviors often include drugs or alcohol. Those with avoidant attachment seldom seek help because they don't believe they can trust anyone to meet their needs.

Finally, there is *disorganized* attachment. This type results from abusive relationships with caregivers, who may have repeatedly raped, physically beaten, or otherwise terrorized the child. To cope with this trauma, the child often dissociates (psychologically separates themselves off) from their primary personality in order to block out whatever is happening. As a result, the child expresses odd or ambivalent behavior toward the caregiver, perhaps running up to seek comfort, but then as they get near, pulling away due to fear. As adults, those with disorganized attachment have a difficult time regulating their emotions in social situations, resulting in excessive dependency or aggressive and hostile behaviors toward others. Consequently, they have difficulty forming and sustaining relationships, including a relationship with God.

There are other reasons why you may have trouble feeling God's love, but these are the big five. Regardless of the cause, the only thing to do is hold onto your faith with every ounce of strength that you have, and pray for more faith like the father of the epileptic child did when he asked Jesus to heal his son: "help thou mine unbelief" (Mark 9:24, KJV).

If you don't feel anything, trust that he is there and that he loves you and will see you beyond whatever is standing in the way of his love. Oswald Chambers described the verse "Though He slay me, yet will I trust Him" (Job 13:15) as "the most sublime utterance of faith in the whole of the Bible" (ibid, Oct 31). He also says that "The life of faith is not a life of mounting up with wings, but a life of walking and not fainting" (ibid, Mar 19). Trusting and holding onto God's hand will help you not to faint, especially when the feelings are not there.

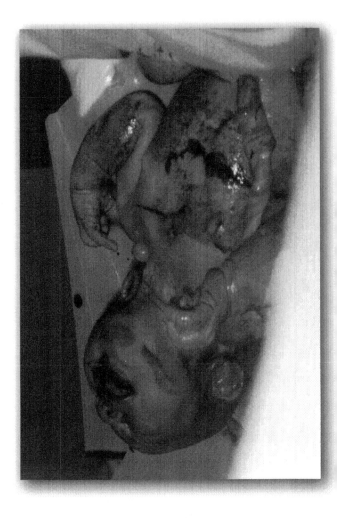

CHAPTER 15

Change Your Mind

§

As I'VE INDICATED THROUGHOUT THIS book, we play an important role in our experience of God's love and favor. I explicitly lay out what that involves in this and the next chapter, and reinforce it in later chapters. If you are Jewish, Muslim, Hindu or Buddhist, I would encourage you to (a) read the chapters in this book that talk about God's love in your faith tradition, (b) meditate on your sacred scriptures, and (c) get together with your rabbi, imam, priest, religious leader or spiritual guide to discuss. If you are Christian (including Catholics, Orthodox, Episcopalians, Baptists, etc.) or have been raised in a Christian home or environment,

Harold G. Koenig, M.D.

this and the next chapter are for you. However, even if you are not Christian or religious, you may still get something out of this material that you can apply to your own faith or belief system.

I've been referring a lot to Michelangelo's painting of God and man on the Sistine Chapel's ceiling (chapter 4). You can't just sit back like the guy in the painting. There are four steps involved in <u>your</u> <u>part</u>. **You've heard it all before**:

1. change your mind (acknowledge & repent)
2. accept God's forgiveness and love
3. be grateful and celebrate
4. love God back

In this chapter, I focus on changing your mind, i.e., acknowledging your errors and blunders, repenting, and pledging to follow a different path. Most people don't get to this point until they are in trouble. If you're at the end of your rope and life is so bad that you just want to quit, you may be there. This is your chance to start over and be reborn into a new life, one much larger and fuller than the present one. As I said before, no one whose natural life is going well, who is content with their present situation, who feels good about him or herself – will want to cast off their old life and take on a new one. Your trauma, tragedy, and pain are what position you to let God change you with his love.

The first step forward, then, is to acknowledge that you're on the wrong path. There are lots and lots of people on this path. The apostle Paul said:

> *There is no one righteous, not even one; there is no one who understands; there is no one who seeks God. All have turned away, they have together become worthless; there is no one who does good, not even one.* (Romans 3:10-12)

Paul is referring to the truth stated in Psalm 14:3, Psalm 53:3, and Ecclesiastes 7:20. The apostle John drills home the point further:

> *If we claim to be without sin, we deceive ourselves and the truth is not in us. If we confess our sins, he is faithful and just and will forgive*

*us our sins and purify us from all unrighteous-
ness. If we claim we have not sinned, we make
him out to be a liar and his word is not in us.*
(1 John 8-10)

Don't call God a liar. Acknowledge that you've
made a mistake in going your own way. Admit
it, confess it – put it all on the table – all of your
anger, resentment, regret, guilt, shame, fear, self-
condemnation, and grievances toward self, others,
and God. Put anything or anyone that you've been
placing first in your life before God on the table.
And then *repent*, i.e., ask God to help you to clear
everything off that table. "Repent" is an offensive
word to many people. Repent, though, was one of
the first words used by both John the Baptist and
Jesus Christ at the beginning of their public min-
istries. The actual word they used for repent was
"metanoia," which simply means "change your
mind" or "change how you think" (Matthew 4:17).

On our own, I'm afraid, we can't get to that
place where we are willing to change how we
think. Therefore, God takes the first step in the

midst of our trauma and tragedy, reaching out to us in that small still voice, wooing us to him as his beloved. Repentance means to feel sorry, true sorrow for being willful, independent, and going our own way. This type of sorrow drives a person to confess their mistakes, admit they are unable to change on their own, and then with God's help, commit to correcting those mistakes. It's a commitment that is renewed every day. This means deciding to think and act differently, and then praying for the strength to do it. Chambers said:

> *Conviction of sin is one of the rarest things that ever strikes a man. It is the threshold of an understanding God…it is not his relationship with men that bothers him, but his relationship with God – "against Thee, Thee only, have I sinned, and done this evil in Thy sight." The marvels of conviction of sin, forgiveness, and holiness are so interwoven that it is only the forgiven man who is the holy man… Repentance always brings a man to this point: I have sinned. The surest sign that God is at*

work is when a man says that and means it...
The entrance into the Kingdom is through the
panging pains of repentance crashing into a
man's respectable goodness. (ibid, Dec 7)

The hardest part is admitting there is nothing you can do to save yourself. Until you get to this point, you may not be ready to fully accept God's transforming love. Chambers said it this way:

The greatest blessing spiritually is the knowl-
edge that we are destitute; until we get there
Our Lord is powerless. He can do nothing for
us if we think we are sufficient of ourselves; we
have to enter into His Kingdom through the
door of destitution. As long as we are rich, pos-
sessed of anything in the way of pride or inde-
pendence, God cannot do anything for us. (ibid, Nov 28)

At the bottom point in my life, I came to realize this truth. It was a painful process -- like being born again -- and the beginning of a total transformation.

CHAPTER 16

Accept, be Grateful, and Love Back

§

AFTER YOU ACKNOWLEDGE AND REPENT, the next step is to accept God's forgiveness and love. If repentance takes a lot of courage, acceptance requires even more. Make peace between you and God. End the war. As you accept his forgiveness and love, give up the guilt, the shame, the self-condemnation. Doing that, however, may be surprisingly hard. We hold onto these toxic emotions tightly, even though they drain us of life. So pray for help. Take him up on his offer: "For I am the Lord your God who takes hold of your right hand and says to you, Do not fear; **I will help**

you" (Isaiah 41:13). That's a promise, and no one is more reliable than God.

However, some think that God is mad at us. He's not. He knows how weak and powerless we are. Like the father in the story of the prodigal son (Luke 15:11-24), he is waiting with open arms, waiting for his son or daughter to come home. He is ready and eager to celebrate our homecoming. We are all prodigal sons in one way or another. Take the risk. Be brave and take him up on his offer.

Once you've accepted God's forgiveness and love, you are then ready for the third step: be grateful. When you fully realize the magnitude of this tremendous gift, and begin to experience the transformation that God's love produces, overwhelming gratitude is the only possible response.

Thanks be to God for his indescribable gift! (2 Corinthians 9:15)

The psalmist expressed it this way:

I will sing of the Lord's great love forever; with my mouth I will make your faithfulness known through all generations. (Psalm 89:1)

Praise the Lord. Give thanks to the Lord, for he is good; his love endures forever. (Psalm106:1)

I love the Lord, for he heard my voice; he heard my cry for mercy. (Psalm 116:1)

This is indeed a time to celebrate and rejoice. Like the psalmist says, you've been <u>heard</u>. The gratitude that follows your acceptance of God's love to remake you is a taste of heaven. It is assurance that you are on the right track, and is usually accompanied by an experience of deep joy. But then the hard work begins. As God's beloved, you now have to start acting that way. God is ready to move heaven and earth to assist you.

The fourth and final step is to love God back. The gratitude that results from receiving and experiencing God's love should produce a desire to act on the FIRST commandment (the same one in all three monotheistic faith traditions):

> *Then one of them, which was a lawyer, asked him a question, tempting him, and saying, Master, which is the great commandment in the law?*

> *Jesus said unto him, Thou shalt love the Lord thy God with all thy heart, and with all thy soul, and with all thy mind. This is the first and great commandment.* (Matthew 22:35-38; repeated in Mark 12:30 and Luke 10:27)

Jesus is quoting Moses from Deuteronomy:

> *And now, Israel, what does the LORD your God ask of you but to fear the LORD your God, to walk in obedience to him, to love him, to serve the LORD your God with all your heart and with all your soul, and to observe*

the LORD's *commands and decrees that I am giving you today <u>for your own good</u>? ... The Lord your God will circumcise your hearts and the hearts of your descendants, so that you may love him with all your heart and with all your soul, <u>and live</u>.* (Deuteronomy 10:12-13; 30:6)

Moses was simply restating the 1ˢᵗ of the 10 Commandments:

I am the LORD *your God, who brought you out of Egypt, out of the land of slavery. You shall have no other gods before me* (Exodus 20:2-3)

This commandment was later also emphasized in the Qur'an:

He is God; there is no god but Him; all praise belongs to Him in this world and the next... (28:70; also see 2:163, 3:64, 6:1, 17:23, 21:25, 42:11, 47:19, 112:1-4, and many other verses)

Notice the language in Deuteronomy above (underlined for emphasis). It's for "your own good" that you do this. It's so that you may really "live." Indeed, he has brought us out of the land of slavery – slavery to our own passions, desires, and addictions. This is how you become free ("unattached" to the things of this world in the Buddhist tradition and relieved of suffering). That commandment was meant for those during the millennia of the past. It is meant for those in the millennia of the future. It is meant for you and I today, whether you are Christian, Jew, or Muslim.

Your part, then, is to acknowledge you are on the wrong path (confess) and change direction (repent), accept God's forgiveness and love, be grateful, and begin to love him back by placing him first in your life, right where he belongs. This is not a single act that is done once and never repeated. No, it is a process that is consciously performed over and over again every day until it becomes a habit, one that you will engage in for the rest of your life.

CHAPTER 17

The Relationship Forms

§

LET'S ASSUME THAT YOU HAVE decided to follow those four steps in the last two chapters and have placed God first in your life. In this and the next three chapters, I describe how to fully experience God's love and sustain it over time.

The process is similar for everybody, although may vary depending on your particular faith tradition or if you don't have a faith tradition. In summary: (1) God reaches out to us; (2) as we listen and respond, a relationship begins to form; (3) as we love God, the relationship deepens; (4) as we begin to love others unselfishly, a reinforcing cycle develops where God pours his love into us, we love others, and others love God (the Circle); and (5) we are sent out into the world to change it. The goal of all this is to live as God's beloved and increasingly experience God's *favor* in all that we do. **There it is**. In this chapter, I focus on God reaching out to us and our response as a relationship begins to form.

We are first loved by God. The New Testament confirms this for Christians: "We love because he first loved us" (1 John 4:19). God takes the initiative. He makes the first move. The starting point is his love for us. He reaches out and calls us in a variety of ways, sometimes prompting us through our thoughts, sometimes during our interactions with others, and most often through our circumstances. He may speak our name in a gentle and quiet voice. A loud, angry and demanding voice is not God's. That voice comes from somewhere else, not God. His voice is full of kindness and compassion for his beloved.

Our creator knows everything about us, so the way he speaks to us will be unique to our individual disposition and the purpose he has for us. To Abraham, he said: "Go from your country, your

people and your father's household to the land I
will show you" (Genesis 12:1). To Moses, he called
his name from a burning bush: "Moses!" (Exodus
3:4). The prophet Isaiah was so sensitive to God's
voice that he overheard God giving out a general
call: "Whom shall I send? And who will go for
us?" (Isaiah 6:8). Jesus called his disciples Peter
and Andrew when they were fishing: "Follow me,
and I will make you fishers of men" (Matthew 4:19,
KJV). God first spoke to the Prophet Mohammad
through the angel Gabriel in a cave on mount *Jabal
al-Nour*. While the Prophet was praying, he heard
the angel say "Read! In the name of your Lord who
created" (Qur'an 96:1).

Sometimes, God speaks louder than usual to
get our attention. He has to speak especially loud
to those of us who are bull-headed and determined
to go our own way. He had to speak that way to
the apostle Paul on the road to Damascus when
"suddenly a light from heaven flashed around him.
He fell to the ground and heard a voice say to him,
'Saul, Saul, why do you persecute me?'" (Acts 9:3-
4). It is said that when the angel Gabriel spoke to

the Prophet Mohammad, the Prophet responded "I am unable to read!" That was not the answer the angel wanted to hear. So "the angel caught hold of him and embraced him heavily."[1] Some of us need to be visited by an angel or thrown to the ground by a bolt of light to stop what we are doing. Most of the time, God speaks in a gentle quiet voice, thankfully. Personally, I'd prefer to listen to God when he's speaking quietly.

How do we tune into that quiet, gentle voice? We need to be alert and remind ourselves that he is constantly speaking to us, especially when we come to a fork in the road and must make a decision. Recognize the gentle prompting as coming from him, and then listen carefully. That small voice is easily suppressed or ignored, and repeatedly refusing to listen will make it harder and harder to hear.

As in any relationship, there is two-way communication as we respond. Our first action should

---

1 Muhammad Mustafa Al-A'zami (2003). *The History of the Qur'anic Text: From Revelation to Compilation: A Comparative Study with the Old and New Testaments*. Leicestershire, United Kingdom: UK Islamic Academy, pp 25, 47–48

be to *humble* ourselves. When God spoke to Moses he said "Take off your sandals, for the place where you are standing is holy ground" (Exodus 3:5). Moses immediately took off his shoes. No questions asked. This act of humility is crucial and is ours alone to do. God will not do it for us. Humility is what creates the space so we can continue to hear God. If we are full of pride and self-sufficiency, the dialogue cannot continue. As noted earlier, this is why we often don't hear God's voice unless there is trauma, tragedy, and pain in our lives, situations where our self-sufficiency fails. It is then that we become open to new ways of thinking as we seek to reduce the pain. These events humble us, thereby opening our ears to hear God and receive from him. God resists the proud but gives grace to the humble. It is a message repeated throughout the Judeo-Christian scriptures.

> *Because your heart was responsive and you humbled yourself before the Lord when you heard what I have spoken… I also have heard*

you, declares the Lord. (2 Kings 22:19; see also 2 Chronicles 7:14 and Psalm 10:17)

Whosoever therefore shall humble himself as this little child, the same is greatest in the kingdom of heaven (Matthew 18:4; see also Matthew 23:12, Luke 14:11, Luke 18:14, and James 4:10)

Once you have humbled yourself, this leads to further communication. At this point you may share your deepest feelings with God, especially whatever you are struggling with at the time. We make our requests and pleas, acknowledging that we can see only part of the picture and trusting that he has our best interests at heart when responding to those requests. Communicating like this leads to belief, faith, and trust in God, which makes possible an ever-increasing experience of God's love.

In the book *Closer than a Brother*, 17th century French monk Brother Lawrence explains how it works. While in Christian terms, his suggestions are useful for everyone:

St. Paul said that there are three things that last forever: faith, hope and love. My experience is that those three are the permanent elements of any man's relationship with God... Through faith we believe his promises and have hope. Through faith and hope we come to love him and for love of him we want to please him in everything we do. So faith, hope and love combined unite us to the will of God.... We believe in him, and so we go where he leads. He is our only hope, and so we cling to him whatever comes. And we love him, and so set out to please him by what we think, what we say, and what we do. (Winter, ibid, p 60)

As Brother Lawrence says, it's because of God's love for us and our love for God that we try to please him in everything we think, say, and do. That's the target we are aiming for, even if we miss sometimes (well, maybe miss a lot).

CHAPTER 18

The Relationship Deepens

§

HERE I EXAMINE what it means to "love God." Knowing how to do that, and doing it, is what enables the relationship with God to deepen as we experience more and more of his love and return it.

In essence, "loving God" means trusting him enough to do what he says. We make this choice to follow his lead repeatedly until a habit develops. Again, that habit thing. Personally, I haven't found that choosing to obey God and doing it over and over again is easy.

The word "obedience" for most of us in modern society has become a profanity. We want to live free and unrestricted and not obey anybody.

This is why we are often not ready to obey until things get really bad. Obedience, though, is the true expression of love. No obedience, no love. Jesus emphasized this to his followers:

> *If you love Me, you will keep My command-ments.* (John 14:15)

> *Jesus replied, "Anyone who loves me will obey my teaching. My Father will love them, and we will come to them and make our home with them.* (John 14:23)

God never forces us into obedience, no more than he forces us to love him. Our obedience, however, is a big part in this relationship. While God loves us unconditionally, he has set up certain rules to govern our actions. Those rules are called the moral law (see chapter 6). As I said earlier, the moral law does not care what we've been through or what situation we are in. It works the same for everyone. The moral law is an absolute one that cannot be transgressed without paying a price. God knows it and wants to spare us the grief. In his famous treatise, *Sovereignty of Ethics*, Emerson says:

> *How came this creation so magically woven that nothing can do me mischief but myself, - that an invisible fence surrounds my being which screens me from all harm <u>that I will to resist</u>. If I will stand upright, the creation cannot bend me. But if I violate myself, if I commit a crime, the lightning loiters by the speed of retribution, and every act is not hereafter but instantaneously rewarded according to its quality.*[1]

We all resist the moral law. Following it on our own is impossible. But again, we have help. God's love enables us to do that if we make it our goal. Again, it is a process and takes time. The results are worth it.

---

1 Emerson RW (1878). The sovereignty of ethics. *North American Review* 10, 12 (Lectures and Biographical Sketches, pp 175-206)

"Because he loves me," says the Lord, "I will res-
cue him; I will protect him, for he acknowledges
my name. (Psalm 91:14)

Consider Abraham, the father of the great
monotheistic traditions. God blessed Abraham
because he obeyed him, even when it didn't make
any sense to do so. When he was an old man
(age 75), Abraham heard God's call to leave his
father's home to travel to a new and unfamiliar
country. Many of us, whether we are young or
old, are in that same situation. God is calling us
to a place we've never been before. Depressed,
anxious, hopeless – yes, those are familiar places.
But to live a Godly life, **that** is not familiar. That
is scary.

With Abraham's obedience, though, came a
promise. God said he would bless him and make
him into a great nation. Where is God calling you
to go? Go! It will take effort and you might not get
there for some time. Abraham had to wait another
25 years until he was nearly 100 years old when

his "body was as good as dead" and "Sarah's womb was also dead" (Romans 4:19). But he didn't stop believing and didn't let go of the promise.

> *Against all hope, Abraham in hope believed and so became the father of many nations, just as it had been said to him, "So shall your offspring be."* (Romans 4:18)

Oswald Chambers said that obeying God helps to seal his promises to us. Abraham was willing to obey God even if it meant sacrificing his most prized possession, his only son who was to fulfill God's promise to him. It was not until Abraham made that decision and was ready to act on it that it became possible for the promise to be fulfilled.

> *"All the promises of God in Him are yea, and in Him Amen." The "yea" must be born of obedience; when by the obedience of our lives we say "Amen" to a promise, then that promise is ours.* (ibid, Nov 17)

We must voluntarily choose to obey. God is our master, but we are not mastered by God. What is the difference between "having a master" and "being mastered"? The difference is love. You have no choice in a relationship where you are being mastered. We are his beloved, not his servants or slaves, and so have a choice in the matter. Listen to what Chambers said about this:

> *To have a master means that there is one who knows me better than I know myself, one who is closer than a friend, one who fathoms the remotest abyss of my heart and satisfies it, one who has brought me into the secure sense that he has met and solved every perplexity and problem of my mind. To have a master is this and nothing less...* (ibid, Sept 22)

Chambers says that obedience is based on relationship. The illustration he gives is that between a son and his father. The kind of relationship God wants with us is centered on that kind of love and mutual respect. We obey God as a result of his love for us and our love for him. As Brother Lawrence said, if we really love someone we will <u>want to</u> act in a way that pleases them. God wants us to obey him because he wants us to flourish in this life. That is real love.

CHAPTER 19

Loading Others

Loving Others

§

Developing a deep loving relationship with God and experiencing more and more of his love are closely related to how we treat other people, particularly those having a hard time in life – those reaching out in desperation as they drown in the depths of despair, confusion, intolerable pain, frustration, anger, loneliness, or misunderstanding. All of us are in that place to some degree, sometimes reaching out for help and sometimes not, perhaps concluding that we cannot be helped. Accepting God's love and following his lead, though, **can help**. And where is he leading us?

When asked by an expert in the Jewish law what the greatest commandment in the Law was, Jesus responded by saying that it was to love God above all else. However, he quickly followed with the second greatest commandment:

> *And the second is like unto it, Thou shalt love thy neighbor as thyself. On these two commandments hang all the law and the prophets.* (Matthew 22:39-40)

There is an order here. Jesus indicated that the second greatest commandment is like the first (i.e., "like unto it"). But it is not the first. The second comes after the first. What does that mean? You can love others unconditionally and unselfishly in the way that God loves them only after you've made God the most important person in your life. It is the love relationship between you and God that enables you to love your neighbor. It is only the experience of God's love from that relationship that makes it possible for you to love others without conditions.

The implications of this are astounding. You can now love others without really needing anything back from them. Others' love is nice, but you don't need it because you've got God's love. God's love fills up your tank and keeps it full, and so eliminates the desperate need to be loved back by people in your life. Now, you can share God's love in an unselfish manner without expectation of return.

Again, Jesus made it clear to his followers what he expects:

> *A new command I give you: Love one another. As I have loved you, so you must love one another.* (John 13:34; see also John 15:12 and John 15:17)

Despite all our religious arguments about the minute details of correct doctrine, all agree on this point. Whether you are Christian, Jewish, Muslim, Hindu, Buddhist, or Humanist, your tradition supports what Jesus is saying. Yes, motivations may differ, but the bottom line is the same. We are here on this earth to love and care for each other. One of Jesus' closest friends, the apostle John, said:

> *No one has ever seen God; but if we love one another, God lives in us and his love is made complete in us* (1 John 4:12).

He goes further:

> *Whoever claims to love God yet hates a brother or sister is a liar. For whoever does not love their brother and sister, whom they have seen, cannot love God, whom they have not seen.* (1 John 4:20)

If we say we love God and don't love each other, then John calls us liars! He insists that we cannot love God if we do not love each other.

For those who believe in and love God, then, our primary goal is to be merciful and compassionate like God is. And he provides plenty of opportunities for that. God's love is so great that it cannot be contained within a person and hoarded. It has to flow through us. In other words, to continue to experience God's love, you have to pass it on. Loving others keeps the flow going. When you stop doing that, the flow stops and the experience of God's love diminishes. As I said above, there is no world religion I know that doesn't emphasize love and compassion as a central teaching. The only exception is the religious extremist who manipulates God's word for his or her own selfish gain. Indeed, let's all be extreme ––radicalized if you wish— but extreme and radical in loving our neighbor.

But, who is our neighbor? Jesus was asked the same question. He responded by telling a story: the parable of the Good Samaritan (Luke 10:25-37). Jesus' answer was totally radical for the people of his day. A person was considered "in" or "out" based on their religious beliefs and ethnic background. Jesus challenged that tradition by saying that one's neighbor is EVERYBODY. That means members of your religious faith who believe like you do and members of other faith traditions who have different beliefs. EVERYBODY. We are to love every person in the same way that God loves them. Admittedly, that is a high bar to reach. But with God's love... all things are possible.

Here is a visual depiction of how God loves us, how we respond to God's love by loving others, and how others experience God's love and love God in return, which keeps love flowing around the circle.

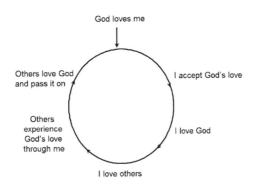

God's love is different from the love most of us are familiar with. God's kind – selfless, unconditional love (sometimes called "agape" love) is the kind that loves the unlovable, i.e., those who cannot love back. This kind of love is *not natural*. This type of love doesn't come from us. The kinds of love that come from us are called "eros," "storge," and "phileo." Eros love is natural sexual love. Storge love is the natural love between parents, children, and family members. Phileo love is love between good friends who are not related to us. Sadly, all forms of natural love are selfish. When we love naturally and people don't respond the way we want, we get upset and can no longer love them. Natural love is limited.

Not so with Divine or agape love. Agape love, which comes from God, is the kind of love that enables us to fulfill Jesus' command to love our enemies, i.e., those who intend us ill-will, wish to hurt us, or have hurt us. Jesus is pushing us out of our natural love. Loving your enemy seems ridiculous and impossible according to the world's standards, or even our basic instincts. To do it we need God's kind of love. However, as I indicated before, we can't give what we don't have, and that's why God has to initiate the process by loving us first. God wants everyone to experience his kind of love, and he is constantly seeking those who will spread that love and compassion. A world full of hurting, disillusioned, and confused people needs it.

So, if you are loved, you have to do something about it. God's love for you *must flow through you* around the **Circle**. With the experience of being loved by God, you will usually want to share it with others. However, there may also be times when you don't feel like loving others. That is when you must make a decision to do it anyway because of God's love for you and your love for God. When you unselfishly love people, you treat them in the way God intends. This may result in people appreciating and loving you back. But maybe not, and that is not your goal.

Your goal is to get them to experience God's kind of love. When others experience God's love through you, they become more able to love God and other people. The experience of unconditional love from you makes them wonder why. Why would anyone love me without conditions or love me if I don't love them back? When they ask, you can then share why you are doing this, i.e., out of God's love for you. The taste of God's unselfish love through you will create a hunger for more of God's love in them.

There is one caveat that needs mentioning here. Loving others unconditionally (and loving one's enemies) does not mean allowing others to hurt or abuse you. Remember, in the second great commandment Jesus says to love your neighbor "as yourself." You are to treat yourself with love and respect just as you are to treat others. Sometimes that requires setting limits or boundaries with others who are trying to harm you or not showing you the respect you deserve as a human being created in God's image. Allowing someone to abuse you is not an act of love for either yourself or the other person.

CHAPTER 20

God's Favor

§

LOVING AND SERVING OTHERS CAN'T occur in isola-
tion. In a society like ours that is anti-institutional,
though, people don't like the structure and rules
of religious organizations. Nevertheless, loving
others often requires a faith community or group
of people (religious and/or secular) where there
are opportunities to love and serve others. That
includes loving and serving the unpleasant, con-
trolling, and wounded people who make up these
groups. Jesus said, "If you love those who love you,
what reward will you get?" (Matthew 5:46). Faith
communities provide the organization and structure where loving others with God's love can take

place, both within the congregation and outside of the congregation. Again, God's love is what enables us to get involved (Psalm 5:7). That includes those of us who are introverted and anti-social by nature. Speaking specifically to Christians, but relevant to non-Christians as well, the apostle Paul says that we were created for good works of service to others and will experience our greatest fulfillment when engaged in that service (Ephesians 2:10). Beautiful things happen when we love God by loving others with God's kind of love.

But, there is more. There is God's *favor*. Remember, God loves us no matter who we are, what we have done, what our religion is, or whether or not we even believe in him. It's a matter of who God is. God's nature is to love each of us with a love that is personal, unique, and unconditional. However, just like we may not always experience God's love, the same is true for God's favor. One reason for that is not being aware it's even available. Do you realize that God's favor is available to you? God is waiting to shower you with it.

However, there are certain things that you must do in order to experience that favor. God wants to distinguish us with his favor, but he can't do it alone without our help (just like God can't force us to love him without some action on our part). One of those actions is preparation. Preparation involves training. God gives us the talents and the opportunities, but it's our responsibility to refine those abilities and make them ready for use when the opportunity arises.

Refining and honing our gifts takes a lot of effort, focus and patience. The focus part is tested when too much is happening, i.e., when we are distracted by the daily problems of life or are enmeshed in challenging situations. The patience part, in contrast, is tested when nothing is happening and boredom sets in. It is that boredom -- the unexciting daily walk in life's valley that many of us, inpatient for action, have trouble with. Chambers said "It is the dull, bald, dreary day, with common-place duties and people that kills the burning heart…" (ibid, Mar 22). It's when nothing is happening – those "dull, bald, dreary days" – that we should be <u>training</u>. God is ready to create the circumstances that will hone our abilities and talents so we can use them to serve him.

The type of training we need, though, might not be the type we expect. It often makes no sense whatsoever at the time. Do you remember that old movie, *The Karate Kid* (1984)? The Karate Kid's Chinese master asks him to paint the fence around the master's house. The Kid is so bored. When it comes time for him to fight in the tournament, though, he realizes why the master had him do this. It was the movements of the brush while painting that enabled him to make karate moves to defeat a much larger and talented opponent.

Likewise, in a more recent TV superhero series *Arrow* (2014), the star Oliver Queen is stranded on an island for five years, where he must struggle to survive. During that time he meets a Chinese girl who trains him on how to use a bow and arrow. The training begins by her instructing him to hit the surface of a pail of water with his hand. This goes on for some time, and he gets frustrated because he can't figure out why she is asking him to do this and not teaching him how to shoot. Then, when she finally starts training him to pull the bow and release the arrow, he discovers why. The self-discipline and control he developed while hitting the surface of the water now enables him to master the bow and arrow, making him a very accurate and powerful marksman. He later tries to use the same method to train his student Roy. Unfortunately, Roy is too impatient to train in this way and ultimately suffers the consequences. Without this seemingly senseless training, neither the Karate Kid nor the Arrow would have distinguished themselves. Both kept at it, though, because they had faith in their master. Our master is God and the people God sends to train us. That training is often in unconventional and mysterious ways.

To experience God's favor and to continue to experience it over time also requires that we follow the rules. Those rules are the moral laws I referred to earlier, i.e., all those do's and don'ts. This is part of the necessary training in self-control. Being the Creator, with intimate knowledge on how we are made and how the universe is set up, God knows that certain ways of living naturally result in either failure or success (as I've said repeatedly). God wants us to have success – the kind that will last. We will achieve that success if we play by the rules, adhere to his boundaries, and follow his guidelines – even when circumstances are bad and nothing makes sense. It's all part of the training, and that training isn't fun or easy and results don't happen overnight. Experiencing God's favor, though, is worth every ounce of effort and minute of training.

CHAPTER 21

The Way Forward for Christians

§

THE FACT THAT GOD LOVES us, wants to love others through us, and places his favor on those willing to hone their talents and follow his rules, is essential to know. Here, I summarize and expand on the points made earlier for Christians in order to help find the way forward. In the next chapter, I examine the way forward for Jews, Muslims, Buddhists and Hindus, and for those who may not be particularly religious.

Jesus has opened the door for those who wish to follow him. Walking through that door means: (a) humbly admitting the error of self-sufficiency (a misstep that all members of the human community have made and/or are making), (b) acknowledging you are helpless on your own, (c) repenting for your error to the point of true sorrow, (d) accepting Jesus' sacrifice on the cross that provides forgiveness and eternal life (the Gospel), (e) receiving God's love, grace, and forgiveness, and (f) committing to do everything possible to bring your will into alignment with God's will.

As I said before, it's not an easy path to take. He warned that it was a narrow one (Mathew 7:14). It's also not a familiar one. Before going through that door Jesus opened, as you peek into the room, it appears dark inside. The Gospel makes no rational sense. It seems fantastic, delusional and illogical (1 Corinthians 2:14). The moment you walk through the door into the dark room, surprise! Everything suddenly lights up. Like when you go into a room with an automatic light switch that turns the lights on when it senses movement. With the light on, you can now see and everything starts making more sense. The New Testament says that God is light and in him there is no darkness at all (John 1:4-9; 1 John 1:5).

You have to move into the light. That is where you will experience his love and favor.

While being re-instated with God is free and unearned, there is a cost – one that involves even more than the effort, focus, and patience I described in the last chapter. For many, the cost is too great. Yet, shouldn't acquiring the "pearl of great price" (Matthew 13:45-46) require some kind of radical or heroic action? Otherwise, everyone would have it. Fortunately, God has made it possible for everyone to have it.

The cost of that precious pearl is the right to yourself, to your independence, and to your self-assertiveness. Chambers says:

> *God is justified in saving bad men only as He makes them good. Our Lord does not pretend we are all right when we are wrong. The Atonement is a propitiation whereby God through the death of Jesus makes an unholy man holy.* (ibid, Dec 8)

This is where the battle is won or lost, and is won by choosing to align your choices with those that

Jesus directs. Jesus said "Whoever tries to keep their life will lose it, and whoever loses their life will preserve it" (Luke 17:33). Going through the door Jesus opened means you are leaving the old life behind. Jesus called it being "born again" (John 3:3). You are born again into a new life that is surrendered to God.

The result of walking through that door, then, is the change promised in the New Testament (and foretold in the earlier Jewish scriptures). It is accompanied by the experience of God's love, joy and peace, as your will becomes aligned with God's.

> *But the fruit of the Spirit is love, joy, peace, longsuffering, gentleness, goodness, faith, meekness, temperance: against such there is no law.* (Galatians 5:22-23)

As I said before, the joy of spiritual transformation tends to fade with time. However, it's replaced by a sense of fullness that no emotion can match. It will take time to learn to walk in the new surrendered life, just as a baby takes time to walk, first crawling, then standing and then walking. Yes, and there is plenty of falling too, and the need to get up and try again.

Although this new life involves a different path than the one you were on before, *this particular path* is headed somewhere. The New Testament says that you were **dead** in your sins as you followed the ways of the world in your old life (Ephesians 2:1). Being dead in your sins means that you are adrift in the ocean of life, with emotional ups and downs, not knowing where the shore is. You may be swimming frantically but getting nowhere. In the new life being offered, you now have a compass to give you direction. It will point the direction to shore. It may take a lot of swimming to get there, and you will likely encounter waves, rip currents, and sharks in the waters ahead. In fact, swimming to shore will require a fight like you've never experienced before as you come up against the forces of evil in this world. If Jesus had to suffer, then you will too. BUT now the effort and pain are getting you somewhere, and the burden is nothing like the one before.

*Come to Me, all you who labor and are heavy
laden, and I will give you rest. Take My yoke
upon you and learn from Me, for I am gentle
and lowly in heart, and you will find rest for
your souls. For My yoke is easy and My burden
is light.* (Matthew 11:28-30)

The burden that Jesus places is lighter because you
are not in this battle alone. There is supernatural
help at every turn for the asking (the Holy Spirit),
and there is a promise that you will get to your
goal if you persist in faith and not give up. You also
have a battalion of others – a faith community –
that is fighting with you, and for you, and available
to help (just as you are available to them). If that's
not been your experience in the group you are in
now or were in before (religious or non-religious),
then find a faith community that will fight with
and for you, and then take advantage of the help
there to ease your burden.

Jesus said, "You are the light of the world. A
town built on a hill cannot be hidden" (Matthew
5:14). The town is the Christian faith community.

The hill is the life built on God's holy words, the words that repeatedly direct us to love God and love people. Believe me, this new life is a whole lot better than the old one.

CHAPTER 22

The Way Forward for Non-Christians

〽

IF YOU ARE NOT A Christian, I believe that God is speaking to you in the language of your own faith tradition. As I've emphasized before, God speaks to people in a way they can understand. He usually speaks to us in the language of the particular historical and cultural context in which we were raised, which is unique to every person. I think God has a plan for those outside the Christian church, since all are his beloved, not just Christians. He wants eternal life for everyone (1 Timothy 2:4-6). I believe that God's message to members of other world religions (and to humanists) is similar to his message for Christians.

God spoke to Jews through Moses and the prophets, where the central message was love God, love the stranger or foreigner, and love your neighbor.

> *The stranger that sojourneth with you shall be unto you as the home-born among you, and thou shalt love him as thyself; for ye were strangers in the land of Egypt: I am HaShem your G-d.* (Vayikra 19:34; see also Vayikra 19:18 and Devarim 10:19)

God spoke to Muslims through the Prophet Mohammad in the Qur'an. The message was to surrender the will and submit life to one God (21:105). Doing good to others, as noted earlier, is also a central theme in the Qur'an:

> *Spend in God's cause: do not contribute to your destruction with your own hands, but do good, for God loves those who do good* (2:195; see also 16:90)

Each community [Muslims, Christians, Jews] *has its own direction to which it turns: race to do good deeds and wherever you are, God will bring you together* (2:148).

God spoke to Hindus in the Vedas, Upanishads, and especially the Bhagavad Gita. *Hinduism Today*'s founder, Satguru Sivaya Subramuniya-Swami, put together a list of the nine basic beliefs that are shared by most Hindus.[1] Three of those are:

* *All Pervasive Divinity: Hindus believe in a one, all-pervasive Supreme Being who is both immanent and transcendent, both Creator and Unmanifest Reality.*

* *The Laws of Karma and Dharma: Hindus believe in karma--the law of cause and effect by which each individual creates his own*

---

1 Subramuniya-Swami SS (2009). Nine Basic Hindu beliefs. *Hinduism Today* (http://www.hinduismtoday.com/modules/smartsection/item.php?itemid=3106)

> *destiny by his thoughts, words and deeds--and in dharma, righteous living.*
> * *Compassion and Non-Injury: Hindus believe that all life is sacred, to be loved and revered, and therefore practice ahimsa, "noninjury."*

God spoke to Buddhists through the Buddha. The message was that if you attached to or worship anything in this world, then you will suffer. Belief in and commitment to a personal God is not a core belief of Buddhism (although for some Buddhists it may be, see Chapter 10). Regardless, showing compassion and doing good to others was central to the Buddha's teachings. In Buddhism, the word "metta" means loving-kindness, friendliness, goodwill, benevolence, and fellowship. Metta is the first in the Buddha's description of four types of contemplation that focus on our relationship to others. The four types of contemplation are: *metta* (loving-kindness), *karuna* (compassion or pity), *mudita* (being glad at the success of others), and *upekkha* (observing in a state of mental calmness and even temper). Ñanamoli Thera says that whoever practices even one of these four types of contemplation for a single moment "has lived for that moment as do the Highest Gods (the Brahma Deva)."[1]

Consider the words of the Buddha from the Pali Canon as he speaks to his followers (i.e., Buddhist monks who are called "bhikkhus"):

Bhikkhus, whatever kinds of worldly merit there are, all are not worth one sixteenth part of the heart-deliverance of loving-kindness; in shining and beaming and radiance the heart-deliverance of loving-kindness far excels them. (Itivuttaka, Sutta 27)

Bhikkhus, when the heart-deliverance of loving-kindness is maintained in being, made much of, used as one's vehicle, used as one's foundation, established, consolidated, and properly managed,

---

1 Thera Ñ (1994, translator). The practice of loving-kindness (metta) as taught by the Buddha in the Pali Canon (http://www.accesstoinsight.org/lib/authors/nanamoli/ wheel007.html)

then eleven blessings can be expected. What are the eleven? A man sleeps in comfort; he wakes in comfort; he dreams no evil dreams; he is dear to human beings; he is dear to non-human beings; the gods guard him; no fire or poison or weapon harms him; his mind can be quickly concentrated; the expression of his face is serene; he dies without falling into confusion; and, even if he fails to penetrate any further, he will pass on to the world of High Divinity, to the Brahma world. (Anguttara Nikaya, 11:16)

It is clear that the Buddha placed a high priority on loving others, showing compassion, and being glad for others when they prosper. He promises that good things will happen to the person who does this.

Most of the major world religions, then, emphasize the common eternal truths that have to do with loving God and loving neighbor, with the promise of relative peace and joy in this life and perfect peace and happiness in the next for those who act on these truths.

Many Christians believe that only Jesus Christ can save a person and give him or her new life (John 3:3). By his life and death on the cross, I believe Jesus saved **every** human being that ever lived and ever will live (1 Timothy 2:4, 6), whether they know it or not. In *Mere Christianity*, CS Lewis says likewise: "We do know that no person can be saved except through Christ. We do not know that only those who know Him can be saved by Him."[2]

Christians believe that Jesus and God are one and the same. Being saved by Jesus just means being saved by God. It should not be surprising, then, that Jesus' message to Christians is the same one that God has been trying to get across to Jews, Muslims, Hindus, and Buddhists in the language of their own faith traditions. Although humanists and atheists may not believe in God, their traditions emphasize kindness and love toward others and respect for individual autonomy. God loves us

---

2 Lewis CS (1942). *Mere Christianity*. New York: Touchstone, 1996, p. 65

so much that he will talk to us in whatever way he can get through to us.

Admittedly, this view is pretty ecumenical. My personal views on this issue have been evolving and continue to evolve. There is controversy in the Christian world about this, and widespread belief that one must convert to Christianity in order to be "saved" (at least in conservative circles). However, the notion that God is speaking to people in their own language is not a new idea (and goes beyond the belief that "all roads lead to God"). Rather, it comes from the New Testament, and so should not be too disturbing, even to Protestant Christians on the conservative end of the spectrum.

> *What business is it of mine to judge those outside the church? Are you not to judge those inside? God will judge those outside.* (1 Corinthians 5:12)

Christians are called to be witnesses for Jesus to the ends of the earth. To me, witnessing means being obedient to and surrendering to God, loving others, and telling others what Jesus (God) has done in my life if they ask. So, do you have to be a Christian to be a witness? Witnessing doesn't always require words, said Francis of Assisi. However, it does require action. In this case, action means putting God first, surrendering your will to his will, and loving others because of God's love for you and your love for God. For humanists and non-theists, it means showing love and respect to others, whatever their beliefs may be. If we act in this way consistently, whether we are Christian or not, whether we are religious or spiritual, or neither, I think we'll be moving forward.

CHAPTER 23

A Personal Note

HAVING READ THIS BOOK, YOU might like to know a little more about me. I think this will explain where I'm coming from, and help you judge the value of what I've written here.

As indicated earlier, I'm not a theologian and have no theological degrees. I'm a physician and medical researcher, trained first as a family physician, and then later as a specialist treating the medical and psychiatric problems of people of all ages, but especially those in middle-age or later life. My professional background is really not that relevant here, other than as a scientist I've made particular effort to be accurate. More important, though, are my experiences in life, and perhaps my lack of experience. Let's start with the latter.

I wish I could gain credibility with you by saying I've gone through the hellish experiences many of you have endured. I have not. I don't mean I've had no hardships, but just not the kind of difficult situations that overwhelm and para-lyze people, making it difficult to hear anything above the roar of their own pain.

So, here is what I've <u>not</u> experienced.

I've never been to war and served in active combat, or been in a life-threatening situation for hours, days or months at a time – like my dad experienced as a US Army grunt in Europe or my father-in-law fighting the Japanese in the Pacific as a US sailor during WWII. I've never had experiences like my mother's five brothers who served in the German Nazi army (three of whom died on the Russian front). I've never had experiences like those of hundreds of thousands of U.S. Veterans who served in Korea, Vietnam, Afghanistan, Iraq, or other war-torn areas of the world.

I've never been addicted to drugs or alcohol, or known the desperation of someone withdrawing from these substances, willing to do anything to relieve the craving and stifle the pain.

I've never been physically hungry for long periods of time, afraid I would starve, or had to endure watching a parent, spouse, child, or close friend starve. I've never been in a severe car accident, major earthquake, tornado or bad hurricane. I've never been in a situation where I was afraid I wouldn't survive or that my loved ones wouldn't survive.

I've never had to escape from my homeland and migrate to a foreign country, and feel the stares of people, knowing that I was different and didn't fit in. I've never had to face discrimination because of my skin color or ethnic background.

I wasn't born with a crippling medical condition like polio or a chronic mental disorder like schizophrenia or bipolar disorder that interfered with my education, work, and social relationships. I've never experienced severe pain to the point of exhaustion, where I was unable to endure it any longer after days, months or years of suffering.

Even my childhood was pretty good. I wasn't deserted by either parent, nor did I lose them to an untimely death. I was never orphaned or sent away to school when I was young and vulnerable. I was never emotionally, physically, or sexually abused by a parent or relative. I was an only child, and so never had a sibling who was favored or someone I had to compete with for my parents' love and attention. I never felt neglected.

Indeed, quite the opposite. I was born generally healthy with a number of physical and intellectual talents. Although my father was a bit distant, he was a hard worker, faithful to my mother, and took time to play with me on Sundays and holidays. I knew my mother really loved me. As her only child, I was the focus of her love, attention, hopes, and dreams. My parents trained me to work hard and made sure I had a good education (both religious and secular).

What is the bottom line? If God met up with the devil to discuss the events happening on earth, he would not brag about me like he did about Job (I hope God learned his lesson with Job):

> Then the LORD said to Satan, 'Have you considered my servant Job? There is no one on earth like him; he is blameless and upright, a man who fears God and shuns evil'
> (Job 1:8).

Satan's response is revealing:

> 'Does Job fear God for nothing?' Satan replied. 'Have you not put a hedge around him and his household and everything he has? You have blessed the work of his hands, so that his flocks and herds are spread throughout the land'... But now stretch out your hand and strike everything he has, and he will surely curse you to your face (Job 1:9-11).

I hate to think how I would respond if God allowed Satan to do that to me. I'm afraid I'd curse God to his face. I hope not. Some of you, like Job, may have felt like cursing God and cursing the day of your birth. Many have certainly asked the agonizing question "Why?" when bad things have happened and there has been no way out.

Having heard my story so far, you might be tempted to think, "How can I relate to anything this guy says? He is nothing like me." Yes, I can understand that, but there is a part 2 to the story.

I struggled through the first 32 years of life trying to figure out my purpose. Initially, I thought it was to succeed in my profession, find a cute girl, get married, and live happily ever after like in the movies. I am by nature somewhat sensitive, anxious, obsessive, and introverted. These characteristics have been both a blessing and a curse. On the positive side, being sensitive has allowed me to tune into people's feelings, which has helped in my family and professional life. Being obsessive and exact has benefited me as a physician and research scientist, professions that require precision and attention to detail.

There have also been some negative consequences to these traits. With a sensitive and anxious disposition has come vulnerability. Growing up, I desperately wanted to please my parents and teachers by working hard and doing what they asked. I became familiar with failed relationships in my early adult life, including a troubled marriage and a painful divorce, and have continued to have challenges in my current marriage. I joke with my wife that during our 30-year marriage we hold the Guinness Book of World Records' record for number of marital counseling sessions, and continue to extend that record.

Another weakness is a tendency toward rebellion. At the age of 18, on graduating from high school when giving the valedictorian speech to hundreds of students, parents and teachers, I had only one message to communicate: "I want to do it my way." I received a standing ovation from my peers, but dead silence from parents and teachers. At the age of 24, I was expelled from one of the top medical schools in the country for some crazy ideas and behaviors. After that I lived on the streets of San Francisco under a building next to Golden Gate Park. When the building inspector finally discovered me after several months, I was forced to move on. Fortunately, I got a job at a car repair shop that allowed me to sleep in the shop's loft. Slowly as my sanity returned, I decided to join the Army. But I couldn't handle that either. The Army rejected me because I wasn't healthy enough, and was discharged from boot camp after two grueling months.

I also struggled with an eating disorder for many years, and while under control now, was a real challenge to overcome. I've had to deal with chronic pain, tendonitis, and disability since my early 30's, and soon after I turned 50, developed chronic eye infections, prostate cancer, and have needed multiple abdominal surgeries for that and other problems. I've learned to live with intermittent chronic pain.

Because of my focused, exact, and driving nature, I've had interpersonal problems at work and home that have created pain and suffering for me and everyone around me. I'm quite impatient by nature, and have had to press on despite frequent boredom and restlessness. While the mountain-top experiences as a committed Christian have been frequent and treasured, I've learned not to depend on them.

As I indicated in an earlier chapter, my lovely wife of over 30 years suffers from a chronic, horribly painful, seemingly untreatable medical condition that affects her mobility and has caused her to mention to me that she longs to be with God. I understand what she means, but that is not easy to hear from your best friend and someone you love, nor is it easy to endure with her the shocking pain that she experiences or the anxiety over the possibility that the pain medication will run out or may someday not help. However, we both believe that what she is going through is somehow fitting into the Divine plan. We remain alert, looking for the good that God will someday produce from these experiences.

Despite all this, I know I'm very fortunate. Sure, I've worked hard and tried to follow God's rules, but to be honest, most of the blessings and favor have been undeserved and unearned. You can readily see why I believe in a gracious and loving God. Since my religious transformation in 1984 my life has become very full, despite occasional adversity. I have a meaningful job, financial security, a loving wife and family, and close relationships with most of my friends and colleagues. All are a direct result of that transformation.

The decision in 1984 to surrender to God was made in the midst of sadness, loss, and confusion. I have been trying to surrender now for over 30 years – successful at times, not so successful at others. As I'm able to do that and follow God's lead, I've found an increasing flow of blessings. Even when I'm self-centered and definitely not surrendered -- even then, while the blessings slow, they still continue. I don't really know why. I can only attribute it to the incredible undeserved grace and mercy of one who understands and forgives.

So, that's who I am and the experiences that've made me who I am. I hope sharing this with you will help in some way, even if you find my life hard to relate to. Like I've encouraged you, my plan moving forward is to "pass it on," pass on the blessings to others and continue to make the hard decision every day to surrender my will to God's.

CHAPTER 24

Final Thoughts

§

MANY PEOPLE – SOME OF you reading this book – haven't been as fortunate as I have. You don't feel blessed or favored as his beloved. If anything, like Job, you feel cursed and abandoned. Are you somehow less deserving of his love and favor than anyone else? NO! You, too, are his beloved, and he wants to place his favor on you. You may not know it or feel it quite yet, but that is reality. The purpose of this book is to help you become aware of that reality – despite all the losses and disappointments you may have had. Those difficult experiences have led you to where you are now, are responsible for the person you have become, and are crucial to becoming the person God intends you to be.

You were never alone and you will never be alone. You are God's beloved, **Really**. God is real and really loves you. He wants you to love him so that his power can flow through you to those whom he puts in your path. His love flowing through you is like no other experience in the world and is worth – a thousand times worth -- surrendering your life to him. I have tasted that love, and I know that once you've tasted it, you will want it too. Love casts out fear. Love heals. Love does just about everything. We need God's kind of love.

So, continually remind yourself as I do that you are his beloved and that his favor rests on you. I continue to meditate on this fact every day, over and over again. I remind myself so I will not forget. I want it to sink deep into my soul and guide the rest of my days. Life begins when you recognize that you are his beloved. I agree with Karl Barth. All the complex philosophical and theological teachings of every faith tradition in the world boil down to one simple message: "Jesus loves me this I know for the Bible tells me so."[1] I'm betting the farm on it. My hope is that you too will begin to see yourself like God sees you. As a verse in another old song goes, all other ground is sinking sand.[2]

For more information, go to: Duke University's Center for Spirituality, Theology and Health: http://www.spiritualityandhealth.duke.edu/. For more information about the author, go to:http://www.spiritualityandhealth.duke.edu/index.php/harold-g-koenig-m-d.

1 If you are not Christian, insert your Prophet and Sacred Scripture here
2 *My Hope is Built on Nothing Less* by Edward Mote, 1797-1874

Made in the USA
Middletown, DE
21 June 2016